Unimaginable

Life after baby loss

BROOKE D. TAYLOR

Printed in the United States of America

First Printing, 2021

ISBN 978-0-578-84945-4

This book is for my first daughter, my sweet Baby Duck,
Eliza Taylor Duckworth.

The breaking of so great a thing should make
A greater crack.

—William Shakespeare

Unable are the loved to die—for love is immortality.

—Emily Dickinson

PART ONE

MY HEART BREAKS

CHAPTER 1

There is no way to begin without telling you the saddest part of the story. It's a love story, and it begins with a positive pregnancy test. It doesn't end with a baby, though. At least not the way I thought it would. My baby died, and I suddenly found myself having to live a life I couldn't imagine.

I had fallen in love with the idea of this baby before she ever existed. I'd been imagining our baby long before I got pregnant, as we daydreamed and saved money and waited for the "perfect time" to welcome our "perfect baby."

I was finishing my graduate program in English literature. My husband was teaching and working on a graduate degree in education. We had been married six years. We'd stretched our shoestring budget to travel. We bought a little house, we had two little dogs, and now we were totally ready to be parents. I began preparing for motherhood the way I prepared for everything: by reading. I read books on pregnancy, natural childbirth, nutrition, breastfeeding, baby sleep, baby food, baby milestones. If I could have tested my way into motherhood, I definitely would have.

It took us a few months to get pregnant, and I fretted and worried until I saw those two pink lines. It was a Sunday morning—Mother's Day. My period was late—finally—and when the test was positive I was absolutely elated. I was thrilled to be pregnant, of course, but I was also so glad that I had forced myself to wait and test Sunday morning. It was Mother's Day—*Mother's Day*!—what a great story to write in Eliza's baby book.

My perfect pregnancy was off to a perfect start. Her name would eventually be Eliza Taylor Duckworth, but before she was born we called her "Baby Duck."

Here's a belief that was shattered: I believed that we deserved this perfect baby. My life was privileged, sheltered. I had been lucky enough to believe that hard work and good intentions were enough to get you what you wanted out of life. I knew, of course, that bad things happened to good people, but I mostly subscribed to the idea that the world was a meritocracy. David and I were good people. We intended to be good parents. We were kind, responsible, smart, and we planned ahead. Surely we would get the baby that we deserved. I didn't even think that much about it, honestly. Once I got pregnant, and then got through the first trimester, it seemed obvious that we would be bringing this baby home.

I was six and a half months pregnant the day my husband got a phone call from Dennis, his best friend from college. I was standing in our tiny kitchen, leaning on the counter next to the fridge. David lowered himself onto a stool at our kitchen island. He answered his phone with a jokey greeting. Then he cleared his throat, his laughter abruptly choked into silence. I turned to look at him, and I watched as the color drained from his face.

Dennis and his wife, Lindsey, were expecting twins—a boy and a girl they named Max and Mia. They were due right around the same time that we were expecting our first child. Over the summer, we'd spent time together discussing pregnancy and planning for how much our lives were going to change. The last time I'd seen them we had talked about nursery décor for the twins. At the time of the phone call, Lindsey was 28 weeks along. It was too early. My breath started coming fast as I listened to David's side of the conversation, a knot forming in my stomach behind my protruding baby bump. After a brief exchange, David hung up the phone and turned to me. His voice was quiet as he told me that Lindsey was in the hospital and one of the twins didn't have a heartbeat. They were doing what they could to keep the other baby safe, but Max was gone.

My eyes filled up with tears. I was devastated for Dennis and Lindsey. I thought about how frightening and heartbreaking it would be to get this far in pregnancy and then not get to bring home your baby. It was terrible to contemplate. I wasn't an idiot and I had done lots of reading. I knew that miscarriages and even stillbirths happened. I knew that not every pregnancy ends in a healthy child. Still, Lindsey and I had been counting down the weeks together since our first trimesters and it seemed like such a cruel twist of fate to get past the first trimester and then past viability—that seemingly dependable 24-week mark—only to lose your baby.

I rubbed my belly as I leaned against our kitchen island. My tears spilled over.

"I can't even imagine," I said to David.

What I meant was, "This is so horrible that I don't want to think about it. I hate that Dennis and Lindsey have to go through this. And also, this is so terrible that I want to distance myself from their pain and suffering. I don't want to put myself in their place. I don't want to consider that the precautions I'm taking might not be enough to protect my baby."

We often refer to losing a child as "unimaginable." And I understand the way this means that it is so horrifying, so terribly unfair, so painful to contemplate that we are trying to make space for the enormity of grief by calling it "unimaginable."

But after my own life crossed the line from what I expected to what I hadn't been able to imagine, the word hit me differently. The other thing I heard when people said this was that they wanted to close off their imagination from the reality of my experience.

They didn't want to imagine what it would be like because it was too uncomfortable for them, because it hit too close to home, because I was the embodiment of their worst fear come true. It made me feel like a social pariah, like a walking specter that made people want to look away.

Here is how you imagine it, I wanted to say. Imagine you've joyfully prepared for months to welcome your baby home. Imagine you've registered for practical baby items and purchased some frivolous but darling clothes to hang on baby-sized hangers. Imagine your husband has put together a crib. Imagine your mother has purchased a car seat. Imagine your friends have thrown you a party and showered you with gifts for your baby. Imagine you go to the hospital, you experience every painful, breathless moment of labor and delivery. Now imagine it was all for nothing and you come home empty-handed.

The truth was, I could easily imagine things going sideways in the worst way possible, but I didn't want to let my brain go there.

Nobody wants to think about their baby dying. Nobody wants to consider that possibility.

But when I said, "I can't even imagine," I also meant, "What Dennis and Lindsey are going through is so huge and painful and terrible that I don't want to pretend I can guess what it is like for them. I don't want to downplay their pain by suggesting that I can imagine the kind of suffering that is now part of their reality, especially since I have suffered so little in my own life."

And, an impulse of self-preservation: "I need some distance from this. I need to feel sure that it can't happen to me."

I will now confess that a small, twisted part of me thought that our friends' tragedy might keep us safe. I had read about the statistics, and the odds were overwhelmingly in our favor. Now we knew someone, were close with someone, who had tragically fallen on the slim side of those odds—I mean, what were the chances that David *and* his best friend would both experience the loss of a child within a few weeks of each other? Statistically, we had to be safe.

Of course, I wasn't taking any chances. I knew that there were dangers and heartbreaking outcomes were possible, but none of the pregnancy books I read dwelt on them, so the odds seemed to be strongly in my favor. Besides, I was cautious and I was careful. I'd been taking prenatal vitamins for months. I had excellent medical care, and my doctor and I had no reason to believe that anything would go wrong. I didn't smoke or take drugs. I didn't engage in risky behavior. I eliminated all alcohol from my diet. I ate healthy foods. I modified my vegetarian diet to eat more protein. I did prenatal yoga. I bought organic produce. I practiced a guided meditation for pregnancy each night before bed. I said my prayers and asked for a healthy baby. I knew that the world was unfair, and that terrible things happened, but I was not pregnant with multiples. I'd had no indications of a problem, no heartbreaking results from a blood test or concerning pictures on an ultrasound. This tragedy had come out of nowhere for our friends, but I had no reason to think that it could happen to me. Since Dennis's phone call, I worried about how he and Lindsey were coping. I hoped that little Mia in the NICU would be okay (and she was), but I had no reason to worry for myself.

I was convinced that the universe was on my side. While I sympathized with our friends' tragedy, I remained optimistic that my baby would be fine. Of course she would! I was riding on a wave of privilege and opportunity and support and confidence. As Toni Morrison wrote in her novel *The Bluest Eye*, "If happiness is anticipation with certainty, then we were happy."

Before Eliza died, I knew that life was unfair and tragedy visited good people without warning. I knew these things. I had witnessed it happen to our dear friends. I still didn't believe it could happen to me.

After Eliza died, a curtain was pulled back. Not only was life full of random terribleness, but so many, many people got less than or other than they deserved. I'm a little bit ashamed to say that it took the death of my daughter for me to see the folly of my beliefs. Intellectually, I *knew* that there were people who worked hard and still experienced disappointment and failure through no fault of their own. It wasn't just about child loss. In the years since Eliza died, I've come to recognize the myriad of ways that luck and good fortune was so often built on generations of privilege, that hard work was only part of the equation. But I've also seen that the opposite is true: that no matter how sheltered you are and how wonderful your life, no one is protected from the curve ball of tragedy.

And so it was that in December of 2010, my life was a to-do list that I simply had to cross off in order to get to my due date. If I got all my papers graded, all my laundry done, the nursery fully decorated, the tiny pink clothes organized, the parenting books read, the coming home outfit selected, then I would have earned my way to the grand prize of bringing my baby girl home from the hospital. My doctor had chuckled at the pregnancy planner I brought to each appointment— "The *Essential Pregnancy Planner*," as though the planner was critical for this pregnancy's success. I loved this baby so much that I wanted to give her as perfect a start as possible. I had so much to get done in December, and then come January she would arrive and I would start the new year transformed and ready to devote my time to parenting her. In that first week of December, I was diligently working my way through that to-do list, one organic salad and prenatal yoga class at time, when those early contractions canceled out everything I had planned.

I went into labor with Eliza almost six weeks before her due date. It was a cold Monday. There was no snow yet, but it was promised before the end of the week—final exam period for my semester of teaching college English classes. I was at home grading a stack of essays, watching the clock so I wouldn't be late for yoga. *Real Housewives* played in the background (I haven't been able to watch that show since, which I admit might be considered a silver lining, if silver linings were applicable in such circumstances).

My abdomen had felt a little strange all day, but I thought it was movement—the baby pushing up against my ribs. I'd been taking a Bradley method class for weeks, determined to have an un-medicated labor and delivery (when you're certain your baby will live, such issues seem important). I had read half a dozen books about labor and had studied the various stages, but this was my first baby and she wasn't due for another month, and somehow I wasn't even considering the possibility that I could be feeling contractions. Then, quite suddenly, I was having cramps so intense that I found myself on my hands and knees, gasping to catch my breath. Still, I wasn't completely *sure* I was in labor. None of the books had suggested it could come on so fast, so early. I couldn't believe it. It was December! This was not what we had planned! We had joked about missing the tax write-off because my baby wasn't supposed to be here until the new year.

The fact was, though, that soon I was in a lot of pain. Even though I remained in denial that I could actually be in labor, I was scared that something was wrong. I knew we needed to get to the hospital right away, but I was still confident that somehow things were going to be okay and whatever was happening could be stopped. I wasn't bleeding, so I could tell myself that everything would be fine.

By this time, I was well into my eighth month, and I was focused on a positive outcome and the joys of bringing my baby home. But this unexpected, premature cramping was breathtaking and terrifying, and by the time we were on our way to the hospital, the contractions were nearly unbearable. I clutched the car door handle, gritted my teeth, and willed David to drive faster.

David had thought I was joking at first when he walked in the door and the first thing I said was that we needed to go to the hospital, but when I groaned through another contraction, he quickly realized how serious things were and he immediately helped me get in the car. We didn't bring a hospital bag or anything—somehow, neither of us imagined we'd have a baby that night. David gripped the steering wheel with both hands as we drove out into the freezing cold. He proceeded to get on the wrong highway and drove us a few miles out of the way before we could exit and turn around.

People at the hospital greeted us with excited smiles as we checked into labor and delivery, but I was in so much pain that I was certain something was wrong.

Then I was in a bed, gasping for breath between contractions, and a doctor—not my doctor, he was on his way but hadn't yet arrived—rubbed a wand on my belly, squinted at an ultrasound screen, took a deep breath, and then told me in the kindest, most sympathetic voice that she was very sorry, but my baby didn't have a heartbeat.

I felt the room swim around me, the edges of my sight getting dark and blurry. I was absolutely sure the doctor had made a mistake. It had to be the cramping that was throwing off the ultrasound. I'd just felt the baby moving that morning—hadn't I? But the furrowed brows and sympathetic eyes of the doctor and nurse told me as much as the no-longer flickering heart on the screen. This wasn't something that could be stopped or fixed.

My baby duck wasn't coming early. She was already gone.

Another contraction wracked me, and I turned and vomited. The physical labor pains I was experiencing were suddenly less frightening, as they now felt like manifestations of my emotional state. My baby didn't have a heartbeat? My own heart must be ripping itself apart, all the way down to my guts. This was my body imploding and shutting down. Surely I would pass out from the agony of it all.

It would have been a relief.

Despite my prior assumption that Baby Duck was coming home with us, I knew that babies sometimes die. I just thought that it only happened in high risk cases—like when women are pregnant with multiples. Or to women who had other health issues. Or in cases of drug addictions or women who didn't take care of themselves while pregnant. Or to women who didn't have access to adequate prenatal care. Or to women who were over 45. It couldn't happen to *me*—a first-world, well-educated, twenty-first-century woman in good health who had been going through this textbook pregnancy as though she were looking to earn a baby *and* a gold star at the end. This was the time of Baby Center and Online baby registries and the at-home Doppler. This was the time of the NICU and 26-week miracle preemies. Babies do not die with no warning for no reason, right? I was scheduled for a doctor's appointment the next day. My doctor had literally declared her "perfect" at my last appointment a few weeks earlier. This could not be happening. Not to me.

I had worried about C-sections and NICU time. I worried about jaundice and colic. I worried about birth defects or genetic abnormalities undetected by the ultrasound. I worried about car seat safety and potential choking hazards and what we would do about our small, elderly dog, to whom I was quite devoted, even though she was unpredictably vicious. I had imagined all kinds of "worst-case" scenarios.

But this? The death of my baby? That was still unimaginable.

The reality, though, was undeniable and I was in the middle of it without warning. I delivered Eliza without any medication, as I had always planned, but without the support of my doula, whom I had never found time to call. A nurse had gently suggested I get an epidural, as it would help with the pain. But unlike the death of my baby, the physical pain felt like something I could understand. As long as I could focus on the sensation that my body was ripping apart, I didn't have to think about my heart breaking. As long as my contractions were so sharp that I could only focus on breathing, I didn't have to consider that my baby would never take a breath at all. And in the end, it hadn't lasted long. Eliza was born an hour after I'd checked into the hospital. I slumped in relief when the contractions ceased, and then immediately started sobbing. The pain was far from over.

After Eliza was born, the nurse bathed her and wrapped her up for us. She invited us to help, but I shook my head, unable to take any kind of action in those moments. Eliza smelled of baby lotion when I cradled her in my arms, letting my tears fall on her pastel-striped hat. Later, I watched numbly from the hospital bed as my husband held her tiny, swaddled body and bent his head over her, crying as he rocked her. I cried, too, but forced my sobs into silence, tears running down my temples and into my hair, not wanting to disturb David or make him leave our baby to try to comfort me.

The nurse kept telling us she was beautiful, but looking at her tiny face—flat and motionless—shattered me. I wanted to run away screaming. I cradled her because when the nurse placed her in my arms, it seemed the only thing I could do, but I wasn't soaking up those moments with her. My chest felt so tight I had to fight for air. I needed everything to stop. I needed to figure out how to turn back time and make everything work out the way I thought it had been promised to me. I blinked and stared at a baby I scarcely recognized in a life that felt like it was no longer mine, my carefully planned future now nothing but a gaping black hole. I had never felt so lost, so bereft, so alone. I cradled a dead baby in my arms, I handed her off to my husband, and I tried and failed to make sense of what was happening.

I felt almost like I was out of my body, watching myself. I held her and loved on her, but it was like I was on autopilot, going through the motions without letting myself feel anything. I kissed her cool forehead and stroked her tiny, cold fingers. I apologized to her for my greatest failure of motherhood, the failure to keep her alive. I whispered to her over and over again, "I'm so sorry. I'm so sorry, baby." I told her again and again that I loved her.

The truth is, I was afraid of her the whole time. I wish I'd been able to treat her like a newborn. I wanted to see her beauty, but I could only see her deadness. I didn't realize at the time how much of her physical appearance was that of any newborn and how much was that of a dead baby. I didn't know at the time how eerily similar those things are, how thin the lines between birth and life and death, despite the stark contrast between pink and ashen colored skin.

I gaped at the nurse who, in her infinite wisdom and kindness, treated my Eliza as she likely treats every other newborn, holding her carefully and gently, diapering and swaddling her, handing her to me wrapped up like a baby burrito with compliments and questions about who she resembled. I couldn't get past my sense that this was a perverse, twilight zone version of the experience that should have been mine, and I wanted to resist this play-acting, but I didn't know what else to do.

She was my beloved baby girl, but as I held her it was almost impossible for me to see anything but her death. She was so smushy. Her soft, wrinkly skin was blotchy and flaky in places.

Her tiny fingernails were perfectly formed, but they were a dark purplish color because her blood wasn't circulating. Her lips were frightening, so dark, like someone had put gothic lipstick on an infant. Her skin was almost wrinkly—another newborn trait that startled me. I didn't remove her hat. I wanted to keep her warm.

I can't remember if I peeked at her toes, or if I've only seen them since in photos. Did I unwrap that blanket? Or was I too afraid?

When I agreed to have her photos taken, I could not imagine ever wanting to look at them. I didn't know how much I would need evidence of her. I kept thinking of those "morbid" Victorian pictures of dead people. I hated myself for feeling repulsed. I wasn't sure pictures were a good idea, but the nurse—thankfully—assured me that I didn't have to look at them, but this way we would have them later if we wanted them.

When blood oozed out of her teensy little nose (which otherwise was perfect and quite cute), I wanted to scream in horror.

I didn't scream. I grabbed a tissue from the tray table by my hospital bed and I wiped her nose because I'm her mom and when babies are born, so too must be that instinct to wipe whatever drips out of your child's nostril. But it was still terrible—another horrific parody of what I should have been experiencing.

As I held her, gazed at her, I was torn between wanting to memorize everything about her, and wanting to get as far away from the entire scene as possible. There was a moment when her arm shifted and my heart leapt. I was certain, for the briefest instant, that she had moved her hand and that this had all been a terrible mistake. This was how desperate I was to have a different outcome.

I wrapped her tiny, impossibly perfect, unnaturally cold fingers around my finger, rubbing them gently as though I could warm them up. I felt faint again, the room growing dark around the edges. I wished that I could lose consciousness. I wanted to blot out everything, to wake up and begin again with none of this having happened.

I regret how much that tiny baby scared me. She didn't even weigh four pounds. But I was terrified of her.

I wish I had mothered her differently, confidently, purposefully. Everything I did felt tentative, fearful, cautious.

It helps to remember that I did mother her differently,

when she was still alive. I mothered her in every vitamin I swallowed, every bite of organic produce I consumed, every gram of protein I counted, every cup of coffee I quit drinking, every glass of wine I never poured. I mothered her with every mindful breath at every birthing class, with every page I turned in every book I read about pregnancy, childbirth, infancy, and parenting. I mothered her when I selected furniture for the nursery, when we splurged on the perfect rocking chair, when I scoured Etsy for wall art that went with our "baby duck" theme for her room. I mothered her with classical music and meditation CDs and Kegels at every stop light in preparation for her natural birth.

I mothered her with every daydream I had about her—from thinking about winter birthday parties to imagining her first Christmas and first words and first steps and every other milestone I could envision celebrating. I started mothering her when I saw two pink lines on that pregnancy test, and I'd done my best for eight and a half months. Still, when I reflect on those final short hours with her in my arms, I think that I should have done more. Should have done better.

I know that I did the best I could with the resources I had at the time. I did the best I could as a shattered and traumatized individual. But all I wanted was to be a good mom—to make her feel loved and wanted and cared for. She was our dream, and I worry that when she died I didn't do enough to show that. I wish now I had done things differently in the hospital. But I believe she felt my love while she was still growing inside me. I believe that she knew how loved and wanted she was, that she heard our voices, felt the warmth of our hands through the skin of my belly, and sensed how much we wanted her here with us.

But now that she was gone, I wanted to be gone too. I wanted to get out of that hospital room as soon as I could. At some point, I made phone calls and delivered the worst news of my life to our family members and friends, mostly without crying. I was completely numb, functioning on autopilot. We had no family in town, our parents lived hours away, so no one else held her or saw her. I felt so protective of her. My doctor allowed us to check out early in the morning. We hadn't even been there twelve hours.

I knew that leaving the hospital wouldn't fix anything, but I had to get out of there. I had to get away from the heads tilted with sympathetic frowns, from the thoughtfully printed sign on the door of the hospital room that told everyone we were bereaved parents, from the sad eyes of the sweet nurses, from the agony of feeling like my suffering was on display. I felt like all these people—doctors and nurses—were watching me to see if I was okay. I was not okay. I was not okay. And I could not bear to be so not okay in front of an audience. I needed to scream, to rage, to sob until my tears dried up, and I wanted to be alone to do so. I couldn't do it where people could see—not because I was afraid of how I would look, but because there was no display of sorrow that would adequately express this agony.

The kind nurse told me that it was okay to cry, but

I held back sobs until my head throbbed and my throat ached. My grief felt too private, too deep. I quite literally felt like I wanted to die, like I wished it had been me instead of her. Crying wasn't enough. I couldn't do justice to what I was feeling, and at the same time I thought that if I allowed myself to express my feelings, I'd never get control of myself again.

Before leaving the hospital, we got information about funeral homes and cremation and different options. We were so completely overwhelmed and uncertain. My husband was worried about expenses. He was teaching; I had just finished graduate school and was piecing together part time jobs. We had planned for hospital bills, but not for additional funeral expenses. The nurse, so kind and compassionate, told me that the hospital would cremate her and bury her for us if we didn't want to go through a funeral home.

Here is my greatest regret: I regret that we left her there at the hospital to be cremated. We did not bring home her ashes. It is a regret with which I continue to torture myself.

I can see now that in those awful, raw, unbearable hours, I was in denial. I couldn't imagine going to a funeral home to pick up my daughter's ashes. I couldn't believe this was my life. I would not accept this. This was the worst and the hardest thing that had ever happened to me. And I didn't think I could bear to do one more hard thing. I think that an irrational but persuasive and persistent part of my brain thought that if I didn't go to a funeral home, if I didn't plan a memorial service, then somehow my baby would not be dead. I didn't want to make those arrangements because I didn't want her death to be true. I didn't want it to be real. I didn't want to be a person whose daughter's ashes were in an urn on the mantle or in a dresser drawer or wherever the hell it is you're supposed to keep the ashes of your dead child. I did not want to be that person who had a dead baby.

I had thought about and considered every significant moment of Eliza's life—from her first birthday to her first day of kindergarten to her graduation. I'd thought about celebrations and vacations. I never once thought about her funeral.

We did not have a memorial service, and this I do not regret. I did not want to go to my daughter's funeral and so I did not have one. Of course, I felt that my daughter deserved the dignity and respect of a formal service. But I was so desperate to be alone and I could not take the thought of suffering publicly. It was another moment when I felt there would be no way to do her justice, to fully express our love for her, and I knew immediately that planning it would have been excruciating. While I understand that many people find it comforting, even now, I know it wouldn't have eased my pain. Funerals are for the living, and I didn't want to go to my baby's funeral. I would have preferred to go to my own.

It remains the greatest regret in my life that we did not keep her ashes, that, in the midst of my grief and trauma, I didn't make a different decision. I wish I had done things differently. I should have asked for help. I should have let my mom or my best friend make that call. I should have known that someone else would help me carry that burden. I was crippled by my grief. I wanted to run away rather than deal with any of this head on. I didn't know how much I would come to regret that decision—or lack of a decision. I didn't know how much I'd want to wear her ashes in a necklace, how it would occur to me one day that I'd want Eliza to be buried with me in my grave, our ashes mixed together, and how years later I would sob and wail because it was impossible and I had made it so.

Dear friends who have walked this path have assured me, though, that bringing home those ashes or burying them in ceremony is not much of a balm. The agony remains, wherever your child rests. Perhaps I take this guilt and push on it, like a tender bruise, when I need to feel close to her again. Part of the ongoing pain of bereaved motherhood is the sense that feeling close to your baby requires suffering.

I have spent a considerable amount of time and energy (and money) on therapy to help me forgive myself for what I didn't do—what I couldn't do. As my therapist gently reminded me upwards of a hundred thousand times, I did the best I could in that moment. I have come to believe that—I think it's true that as a first-time, shell-shocked, traumatized young mother, I did the best I could, though I know others who did better and I wish I could have been more like them.

I understand now that not having the wherewithal to deal with the aftermath of her death the way I wish I had was not a parenting failure or a character flaw. How could I have better prepared myself for something that should have never occurred? I know my love for her is bigger than any one decision I could make, whether that decision was right or wrong. But I still carry these pieces of regret close to my heart. When I remember that I was in a blind panic, that I was not thinking clearly, when I remember that decision was made in a moment of trauma and fear, I can begin to forgive myself. I regret that I couldn't have done better. I don't let that guilt eat me alive anymore, but I still feel it occasionally, even all these years later, gnawing on my insides.

When I start to exhaust myself with guilt or regret, it helps a bit to remember that if I had the power to turn back time and change history, I wouldn't keep her ashes in an urn. I'd save her life. I hate that I left her, but I hate most of all that she died.

It helps to remind myself that in the time that she was with me on this earth, she was loved. She was warm and safe and wanted and cared for. She was surrounded by the warmth of my body and the beat of my heart. Mistakes I made came later, after she was gone. I can use those to torture myself, but I know they didn't hurt Eliza. She only knew my love.

Her cells still pulse in my bloodstream, her heart is still carried in my heart, her life is still inextricable from mine. She is with me still. When I die, Eliza's name will be etched with mine on a piece of rock. In every way that matters, she will be buried with me. In anything and everything that comes after this life, we will be together.

PART TWO

THE AFTERMATH

CHAPTER 2

As eager as I was to get away from the hospital room, I was running away from the shock only to plunge into the grief. In some ways, my little house provided the same creature comforts it always had—including my two small dogs and comfortable, if ugly, sofas. But it was a house in which we were preparing for the imminent arrival of a baby girl, and everywhere I looked was a reminder of the happy, hopeful, expectant parents we had been just a short time ago. Those items—a car seat still in the box, a pile of tiny pink clothes in the small hamper, a stack of board books—that had made me giddy with anticipation now gave me the feeling of lead sinking in my chest, and somehow I had to sort through and decide what to do with them.

I'd spent seven months of my life obsessively and delightedly planning for a future that included months of caring for an infant. I expected my entire life to revolve around a person who had been closer and realer to me than anyone. Now she was suddenly—inexplicably—missing from my life. My life with her in it had been so close I could taste it—I was going to grade the final papers of the semester, celebrate the holidays with my family, and greet my daughter along with the new year. My vision of it was so clear. The coming year was going to be the best of my life. It felt as though I literally had everything I wanted.

One of the most shocking and confusing things about Eliza's death was that suddenly everything in my life was different but nothing in my life had changed. Except I wasn't pregnant anymore. I was no longer *expecting*. Nothing was different, except that I had anticipated everything would change and now, it didn't.

Instead of having a newborn upend our lives and our routines and everything we did, our lives were exactly as they had always been. And this sameness was sickening. We had been preparing for major shifts in routines, in priorities, in focus, in day-to-day life and long-term plans. After months of expectation and preparation and planning and dreaming, we were left with a room full of baby things and no baby.

We now had the freedom to do anything we wanted. And there wasn't anything I wanted to do.

Occasionally, I'd get distracted by something, and then I'd get the strange sense I should be doing something. If I chased that thought, it would take me back to the lengthy to-do list I'd penned in the back of my pregnancy planner... laundry, nursery preparation, purchasing diapers, scheduling a photographer... It only took an instant for my brain to shift to sickening disappointment. There was nothing left to do. She was gone.

We packed up the nursery almost immediately. I wanted it gone. I could not stomach the notion of a monument to our grief in the form of an empty nursery. Our house was small and the nursery was taking the space of the guest room. There was no point in asking guests to sleep on a futon when the crib could be put away and the guest bed taken out of storage.

Later, I got to know people who left their nursery as it was—a place to honor and remember their baby, a place to visit, to cry, a shrine of love they left in place until it could be used by a younger sibling.

I can understand this now, but my own reaction was different. I wanted to rip our nursery apart. I wanted to throw every baby item into the dumpster, alongside the maternity outfit I'd been wearing on the day I learned my baby was dead. I wanted to destroy all evidence that I had hoped and planned and counted on bringing this baby home. I wanted to chop the crib to splinters for letting me believe that I'd put my baby in it, like every other mom I knew. I wanted to shred the pink clothes with their tags still on for letting me believe that they would need to be washed and folded or hung on tiny hangers in the closet.

Instead, I stuffed everything in plastic tubs and stacked them in the attic.

The day after I got home from the hospital, my college roommate emailed me, awkwardly, painfully apologetic. She'd ordered me a baby gift since she couldn't attend my shower. She'd gotten a notice that it was scheduled to arrive.

It did arrive. I put it away without opening it.

We had to buy big plastic bins—or maybe we asked my parents to bring them. We filled them with tiny pink clothes and yellow stuffed ducks and board books and boppy pillows and *A Nursing Mother's Companion*. It was a bin of broken dreams and I wanted to get them put away as far away as possible. The physical reminders were unbearable. How could I have been so stupid? How could I have purchased a Madonna onesie at Target and assumed that I'd be lucky enough that the baby squirming away in my belly would get to wear it? Every item was a symbol of my hubris, of the pride that came before my fall. To think that I had already selected a bathtub for my baby with the blind certainty that one day I would put my baby in it!

We'd put a shelf up above the changing table— a place for lotions and diaper cream as well as picture frames and knick-knacks. It was bolted securely to the wall as a precaution for the baby we were supposed to be placing on that changing table.

The baby was gone.

The changing table was gone.

The shelf was now jutting into the room at eye-level, with no furniture underneath it. The guest bed was on the adjacent wall, so the awkward position of the shelf forced us to duck our heads if we wanted to access the far side of the guest bed. It was odd and confusing looking, an empty shelf, randomly placed on the wall, not to mention that having to hunch down and move around it was an annoyance and potential danger. It was absurd. We should have taken it down.

We left it there.

Part of me desperately wanted to believe that the changing table would be back in no time. Surely there was no point in removing the shelf, spackling and repainting the drywall. But I think I also liked how it marked the absurdity of what had happened. How was this possible? How could this be my life? How could I have put up a shelf in a nursery for a baby who would never occupy it? And how could anyone ever expect me to take it down?

None of this made much logical sense. Least of all the death of my baby.

As a childbirth class assignment in preparation for labor and delivery, David carefully wrote out a long list of phrases that he could say to me during labor that would be helpful and supportive (You are a great mom already! Hang in there. You are doing a great job! Baby is almost here!). I had laughed at the idea of him referring to his legal pad while we were in the hospital room counting and breathing through contractions, but I appreciated the gesture.

I found that list a few days after Eliza died. A yellow sheet of paper, folded up with some other items we had planned to take to the hospital. A list of no-longer helpful phrases written in my husband's tiny, meticulous printing.

He hadn't said a single one of those phrases during her actual birth. In shock, he repeated one sentence over and over again: "I love you."

I heard in those words all the unspoken things:

I can't believe this is happening.

I don't know how to fix this.

I am scared.

I am heartbroken.

Please don't die.

It's one of those clichés people say—that they never knew how much they loved their husband until they saw him become a father.

For my husband, the first experience of fatherhood was not a whirlwind of sleepless nights, poopy diapers, and bewilderment about how to support a breastfeeding wife. His first experience was cradling a silent and motionless little infant while his wife choked back sobs in a hospital bed.

I watched him with the baby. I was waiting for a miracle, for her to take a breath, for me to wake up from this nightmare, for time to reverse itself so we could get a do-over, for someone to realize somewhere that there had been a terrible mistake and this was not my actual life. My husband cradled our baby girl and whispered to her. I couldn't hear him but I know what he was saying. It was the same thing he kept saying to me: I love you, I love you, I love you.

All I could say to him was, "I'm so sorry."

I felt like I needed to apologize to everyone—to my husband, to my parents, to everyone who'd given me gifts at my baby shower, mistakenly assuming I would have a living baby. I felt that had failed Eliza and I had failed everyone else who was counting on me.

I wanted to tell David how sorry I was that he didn't get to be a dad the way we had imagined. How sorry I was that I hadn't realized something was wrong. How sorry I was that I couldn't save her. How sorry I was that I had failed at this—the thing I wanted so desperately to get right.

I wanted to apologize to my parents, who were so looking forward to being grandparents. How sorry I was that instead of giving them a grandchild, I was giving them a wreck of a grown daughter to worry about.

I wanted to apologize to Eliza for not giving her the life I had promised. For not being able to keep her. For not doing whatever it would have taken to save her life.

How could I not have known? How could I not have suspected something was wrong?

I was just so damn sorry that everything was wrong and nothing could be fixed.

When I came across David's list of coaching phrases after Eliza's death, it felt like a punch in the gut. (*I'm proud of you. You're doing great! It won't be long now.*) Part of me wanted to crumple it up and throw it away in a rage. Instead, I folded it carefully and placed it between pages of Eliza's mostly-empty baby book. We didn't get to bring our baby girl home, but it wasn't for lack of preparation or effort or desire. That list was one more piece of evidence of how much she was loved and wanted.

David and I loved our baby duck when she was a shapeless bean with a flickering heartbeat on a grainy ultrasound screen, and we loved her when she magically developed into a glowing baby shape with a gorgeous profile and a fist that unclenched itself to wave during her twenty-week ultrasound.

We loved her when she wriggled and kicked inside me, moving enough that he could set his hands on my belly and feel her squirm.

We loved her when she was born still, too pale, with a tiny purple mouth, a silent little form wrapped in a blanket with impossibly soft, frighteningly cold skin. We loved her even as she shifted from the baby who would be to the child who would never see the life we had promised her, who would never live the future that had been waiting for her.

I'm not sure how you love a baby you never knew, except I didn't know how not to love her. We had already dreamed her into life. Loving a baby you don't know turns out to be incredibly easy. Babies don't earn love by taking their first breath or exhaling their first cry. They're born into love. And it turns out that this doesn't change whether they are born living or dead.

Emily Dickinson wrote, "Love is like life, merely longer," and I take comfort in that measure of love's ease and eternity. Love *is* like life, except it's eternal. It happens easily, effortlessly, like breathing. But it doesn't stop when vital signs are discontinued. Life can slip away, but love will go on, spilling into the vast, empty space of who she might have been.

CHAPTER 3

Eliza meant everything to me. She left too little evidence of this behind. I had the material objects that belonged to her, or would have belonged to her—clothes, blankets, furniture. But no one else had experienced her existence in a physical, material way. Not the way I did. Others were anticipating her arrival with great delight, and others would mourn her loss with us and grieve the empty space she left behind. But no one would experience its emptiness quite the way that I would, because no one else had been filled up with her.

I had carried her inside me and now I was left carrying all my love for her, with nowhere to direct it except toward grief. This was supposed to be a new beginning for both of us—her birth, my motherhood. She had been here and she had been so real, so close. I'd felt her living. I'd touched my stomach as she twirled and kicked within. I'd watched my skin stretch to accommodate her growth. Then she was gone. She was still. I was empty. And yet my love was there, turning into this murky pool of grief because it had nowhere else to go.

I expected to feel sadness, grief, and anger after Eliza died. What surprised me was how much shame I felt. When my baby didn't come home with me, I obviously felt devastated. But I also felt duped. I had been robbed of something that I was certain I'd get to keep at the moment when I was least expecting it. I'd been tricked. I wasn't just broken hearted and profoundly disappointed. I was also ashamed and embarrassed—like every pregnant mother, I had expected to bring home a baby, but somehow I was the only one who was an empty-handed fool.

The loss of a child feels like a broken promise. It's grief, but with a sharp edge, breathtaking, amplified, and unending. You feel sorry for yourself, sorry for those who also loved your baby, sorry for the baby who will never get to celebrate a birthday or start kindergarten or lose a tooth or accomplish any of the ordinary delightful milestones of childhood. You feel guilty that you couldn't or didn't do something to avoid this outcome, and devastated that the future you'd imagined was wiped away. You feel ashamed and embarrassed that everyone else figured out how to have a baby and somehow you didn't. You feel lost, angry, confused, shattered. You can no longer trust the idea that the universe is an orderly place where things happen for a reason—maybe you never really believed that anyway, but now you have to face up to the randomness and learn to accept it in a way that you never had to before, back in your old life when only grandparents died and not until they were in their eighties. You miss your baby but you also miss your old self, your old life, and you've been sucker-punched, robbed of something precious that you never believed you could lose.

Our society celebrates motherhood and pregnancy—and by "celebrates," I also mean it sends us an onslaught of marketing and advertisements telling us all the things that we are certain to need in the months to come. We are implicitly reassured that once we reach a certain point in our pregnancy—past the first trimester—then bringing home a baby is basically A Sure Thing. We're told to believe in it, no matter how nervous we might be, or whether our lives have been distantly touched by a stillborn baby. Pregnant women are not asked to imagine the death of their child—they are urged *not* to worry, *not* to stress. Pregnant women should be in planning mode. Nesting mode. Every book, magazine, and website prepares us to bring home a real, live baby. We're instructed to create registries and decorate nurseries and have baby showers and choose names and pack hospital bags. In all these messages is an implicit promise from society at large and from everyone we know that we are going to bring our baby home.

At one point, a few weeks before Eliza was born, the childbirth class I was taking was stressing me out. I was talking to my mom about the pages of reading and worksheets I needed to complete before the next class session, on top of all the reading and grading that I had to do for work. My mom laughed and reminded me, "Even if you don't do your homework, you'll still get to keep your baby."

It was easy to say because we all believed that was true.

Sometimes I think, *Why did I trust that this would work out for me? Why did everyone let me believe that my baby would be alive in the end?*

But also… *How did this* not *work out for me when it worked out for everyone else?*

Of course, I know now even better than I knew then that it *hasn't* worked out for everyone else, but initially I couldn't shake the feeling that I had somehow messed up and lost what everyone else gets to take for granted.

I was ashamed that I had failed where it seemed everyone else succeeded—teenagers have babies! Why couldn't I? —but I was also angry that the world had conspired to trick me into thinking that I would get to keep my baby. Why the hell had Babies-R-Us let me take a scanner around their store? Shouldn't they have told me that I can't be certain this baby will ever come home? What's that adage about counting chickens before they're hatched? Why aren't people saying *that* to pregnant women? I was suddenly baffled by the way my culture blithely celebrates babies with showers *before* they are born. In retrospect, it seemed appalling. How could my dearest friends and family members have thrown baby showers for me when there was this possibility—albeit a one percent chance—that my baby would unexpectedly die in my belly? How could my Bradley class instructor spend hours talking about the physical process of labor and delivery without warning me that my baby might not be alive at the end of it? How could my prenatal yoga instructor let me breathe in and out without telling me my baby might not ever take a breath? How could my doctor call my baby "perfect" at every appointment and not warn me that "perfect" doesn't necessarily mean "alive" after 35 weeks? How could my body expand and morph into a pregnancy that felt both completely bizarre and amazingly natural without giving me a hint that my baby could die and I might not even *notice*? How could my "Mother-to-Be" tea bags offer sweet little sayings on each tag like "Love is the ultimate law of life" and not have a disclaimer: "*Also, your baby might die"?

It took a long time for me to get past this feeling of shame and embarrassment that I had failed to do what so many women appear to do effortlessly, what our culture seems to promise our bodies will do once we see two pink lines on a pregnancy test. I knew that people felt sympathy for me, but I also felt like an object of pity—the kind of person that people felt sorry for and wanted to keep their distance from. The kind of person who must have done *something*—something irresponsible? Something karmic? —to cost her baby its life.

I felt betrayed by my body and my healthcare providers and my yoga teacher and every baby and pregnancy website and all the big box baby stores and hot tea bags. They'd all tricked me. But I was the idiot who had fallen for it. I thought she was a sure thing and then I hadn't been able to keep her alive.

I had spent my whole pregnancy trying to achieve The Best Pregnancy Ever in preparation for The Ideal Labor and Delivery Scenario so that I could then bring home The Most Perfect Child Ever to Exist. When literally the exact opposite of all of that happened, in addition to being devastated, I was mortified that I had believed it possible. I was ashamed of my optimism, embarrassed by my own certainty. I had to expect the worst outcome from now on. After all, to do otherwise would be a failure to learn the most important lesson of my life, wouldn't it?

My therapist gently reminded me on multiple occasions that being hopeful never harmed a baby. But even now I can't cheerfully expect that things will work out in my favor. Perhaps the universe was not hell bent on my personal destruction, but it seemed at best a neutral force at work, completely nonchalant about the hell it wreaks on the hearts and minds of human beings as we try to go about our daily business. At any rate, I will never know why my prayers for a healthy baby were unanswered.

Of all the things that have changed for me over the course of the past several years, this sense of shame is the one that has perhaps shifted the most. I am no longer embarrassed that I fell for the narrative that pregnancy equals baby. How could I not have believed that when there is no escape from that narrative? The certainty of a positive outcome from pregnancy continues to be the prevailing story that we tell. Even now, I find myself echoing that narrative to others. I have come to realize that we tell that story not to fool people into complacency, but maybe as an affirmation that we would like to will into existence.

And although I will always wonder if there might have been something I could have done, I recognize the painful and neutral equalizer of stillbirth and child loss.

Pregnancy loss has affected many more people than we realize, but strength in numbers is cold comfort when all you want is your baby in your arms. And while our numbers may be comparatively small to the number of babies born alive, there is no one exempt from the possibility. Certainly, some of us are at greater risk than others, but the element of surprise makes no discernible difference when it comes to the intensity of grief.

We should all be so lucky as to be caught off guard, to have enjoyed the naïve certainty of a pregnancy and the delighted expectation of bringing home a baby. When it was all over, at first it felt like a cruel joke that I had trusted in my future, but I can finally look back at that pregnancy and my innocence, and find some peace. Believing that everything would be okay gave me the opportunity to love my Baby Duck without reservation or fear.

CHAPTER 4

I would continue to fixate on the question of why this had happened to me, but I also wanted to know more precisely how this had happened. How did a baby who had been declared perfectly healthy a few weeks earlier suddenly *die*? Were there warning signs that had been missed? Were there tests that should have been done? I carried a heavy weight of guilt. I had done my best, but even still my body failed her. How did this happen?

We did an autopsy, drew what felt like gallons of my blood for testing, and sent my placenta to pathology to be examined. We got no clear answers. On the one hand, there was some relief that this probably indicated that my womb was not destined to kill all inhabitants, but the lack of explanation did not seem to exonerate me. I kept obsessing over what I should have done.

I should have done kick counts at 24 weeks. I should have done them more consistently. I should have asked for more monitoring. I should have realized that she wasn't quite as big as she should have been. I should have made sure that I never rolled off my left side while sleep-ing. I should have noticed decreased movement. I should have noticed increased movement. I should have gone to the hospital sooner. I should have sensed that something was wrong weeks earlier. I should have avoided spicy foods. It didn't matter that none of these changes were likely to have made a difference. I should have been able to save her with my love alone.

I wanted desperately to dream about Eliza. Instead I had dreams about eating unpasteurized cheese while pregnant. I woke up sweating. I called my doctor to ask him if I could have gotten listeria from eating queso dip.

My guilt began to ease only when I realized what it meant to blame myself for something that was not within my control. Believing that I could control my unborn child's health and safety through positive thinking and healthy choices—and, honestly, having that idea echoed and affirmed for me by prenatal yoga classes and natural childbirth class instructors—also came with a dark corol-lary. The belief that everything was in my control and I could have changed the outcome implied that all babies who were *not* born 100% healthy and perfect by our general social standards had been somehow harmed in utero by choices made by their mothers. The truth is you can't love a baby into perfect health and you can't control the way DNA lines up as cells divide in your uterus. Of course, there are measures of caution that should be taken and monitoring that can be done, but to trust the narrative that a mother always knows and that our choices are the only things that affect the outcome of pregnancy is a false and destructive narrative. It leaves so many of us blaming ourselves for a twist of fate we never could have seen coming, let alone prevented.

I wanted to give my unborn child every advantage, but if I believed during my pregnancy that I could ensure my baby's health and safety through organic produce and mindfulness meditations, then I was clinging to the false notion that when babies were stillborn or had birth defects or other health issues that their mothers had simply not tried hard enough.

Basic health and quality prenatal care aside, biology, DNA sequences, chromosomes, and teeny-tiny baby organs—these are wild and fragile. We can study, learn, operate, and medicate, but we can't work magic. My efforts to have a healthy and safe pregnancy were not wrong, but they were misguided in the sense that I thought I could earn my way to a baby. When I failed to get the proverbial prize, I felt that it must have been my fault. Why hadn't I been paying better attention? Why hadn't I known that something was wrong?

And yet, I'd thought about her *constantly*. I had talked to her each night. I'd lain in bed with my hands on my stomach, playing Mozart for her, sending her love. I'd laughed out loud when she was kicking so much that my husband's grandmother felt her little foot up by my ribs. And even if I hadn't done those things, I was her mom. She was surrounded by the sound of my heartbeat, the flow of my blood, protected by the strength of my bones and muscles. My body was growing her and nourishing her. The miracle didn't end the way I wanted it to, but that process still mattered.

As mothers, we tend to torture ourselves with guilt. *If only I'd called as soon as I noticed decreased movement. If only I'd not chosen to have a home birth. If only I'd not gotten an epidural. If only I'd been wearing sturdier shoes so I didn't slip and fall. If only I had asked for a C-section sooner...*

Because we had no discernible reason we could pinpoint for Eliza's death, because there was no specific cause to blame, I shifted all the blame to myself. And how could I ever forgive myself for letting my baby slip away?

I could forgive myself only by admitting that I was powerless to stop it.

If I could have prevented her death, I would have. If love had been enough to save her, she'd be here with me. The truth is, no matter what people say, sometimes terrible things happen for no reason at all.

CHAPTER 5

I think that if Eliza had lived, I still would have been mildly horrified by my postpartum body after my first child, but I hope I would have taken it in stride, appreciating all that my body had done to bring a baby into the world. I had done quite a bit of reading about the physical and mental postpartum experience, but there was nothing that could prepare me for the disgust and self-loathing that came with a postpartum body and no baby to show for it. I imagine that, had I gone home with a living baby, I would have been too delighted with her and too preoccupied with parenting to care that my belly still looked 5 months pregnant even though my womb was empty. But I had nothing to take the focus off my suddenly grotesque and unfamiliar body, which had also failed to keep my baby alive. I felt disfigured and disgusting. There was no quick fix for this—so I mostly cried.

Once I got home from the hospital, the tears came so easily that I thought they might never stop. It was like a deluge to confirm the magnitude of what we had lost.

Superficial concerns about my appearance were buried deep under grief for my daughter, but I still couldn't shake the discomfort and uneasiness I felt in my own skin.

My body felt foreign and hideous. I was horrified by the distortions that I otherwise would have accepted as par for the course. Instead, it was insult added to injury that I had to endure these awkward and uncomfortable changes in my body when I didn't get the delightful distraction of a newborn. A living baby would have softened these transformations and made them laughable. But without Eliza here, my bleeding, sagging, lactating body felt like a horror show. Even when I could turn off the replay of those hours in the hospital that looped endlessly in my brain, I could hardly ignore the physical evidence of a postpartum body.

I was left with nothing but the empty shell of myself, and living in my own skin felt unbearable. I had to cope with the bleeding, of course, the lochia that is like a period on steroids. Everyone who has babies seems to gloss over this as no big deal, but for me it was a red mark of failure that required supersized pads in my underwear. I topped the super absorbency with Tucks hemorrhoid pads and kept them in the freezer for relief. I'd read about this on a mommy blog while I was pregnant—it had been a jokey blogpost about building an icy pad like a subway sandwich to sit on. For me, though, as I shoved them in my stretched out maternity underwear, it felt like staunching a wound from which I would never recover, a gory reminder of a battle I had lost.

When my milk came in, it was another trauma.

My body was a freak show. My breasts swelled to the size of volleyballs, hot to the touch and rock hard with breastmilk three days after Eliza was born. They were so swollen and engorged that I couldn't bear for anything to touch them—even the fabric of my t-shirt was painful. I cried so hard I thought I might vomit, and then made myself stop crying because the sobs that racked my chest made my boobs hurt even more. My mom called a lactation consultant to see if there was anything we could do. In the old days, doctors used to give women who weren't nursing medicine to dry up their milk. Evidently that practice was no longer considered safe, but I personally might have taken the health risk, as I slept sitting up in an armchair for three nights because rolling over on my boobs was unbearable. Barely dozing, I stared blankly at the TV into the wee hours of the morning, hating my idiotic body with these monstrous breasts that didn't even know my baby was dead.

I was desperate to do something to reduce the engorgement, but the lactation consultant advised that I avoid expressing milk for relief, because that would only encourage more milk production. In the shower, desperate to deflate the porn-star attachments that felt completely foreign to me, I tried to squeeze my own boob to get milk out of it, but I couldn't figure out how to do it properly and it hurt. I gave up and let my tears mix with the shower, ignoring the advice the same lactation consultant had given to avoid warm water on my chest, as that could evidently encourage milk production as well. (How ironic that while I was pregnant, I had worried about whether I would have a sufficient milk supply and be able to breastfeed; now, all I wanted to do was make this milk go away.) I took Advil to ease the swelling and discomfort and then I tried not to move.

I needed some support, so I wore my stretchiest sports bra (stretching it out well beyond capacity). I put cabbage leaves up against my skin—an old midwives' remedy that did seem to work. In an effort to reduce the swelling, I also put ice packs on top of the cabbage leaves. The coolness offered some measure of relief, apart from the discomfort of shoving ice packs inside an already bursting bra, but despite the ice, the heat of my stretched skin quickly warmed the leaves. I reeked of cooked cabbage, like a sad Irish crockpot. The indentions of cabbage veins pressed into my skin, crisscrossed like scars across my breasts.

I drank sage tea, which was terrible. It tasted like liquefied Thanksgiving stuffing, but I choked down cups of it because I was desperate to get my boobs somewhere close to their normal size again and it was recommended to dry up milk. I can't say whether it sped along the process. At least it gave me something to sip on that felt soothing on my throat, which was sore, my voice hoarse from sobbing. The fact that it tasted terrible also seemed fitting. I drank it like a punishment that I deserved.

My stomach, which had been stretched so taut and cute under maternity dresses was a strange, saggy semblance of its old self, my belly button completely distorted. The small scar from a naval piercing I'd thought was a good idea in my teens was now a divot in my skin reminding me that I used to be a completely different person. The linea negra down the center of my abdomen no longer felt like the mark of motherhood, but like a scar of shame highlighting a task incomplete.

I hated my postpartum body, not because it was not conventionally attractive, but because it was a visual reminder of the pregnancy I'd experienced and the baby I didn't have. I hated my maternity clothes for the same reason. I rarely went outside in those first weeks, but I trekked through our snowy yard and across the icy alley to the dumpster so that I could dispose of the maternity outfit I'd worn the day I went into labor with Eliza. I never wanted to see the pants or shirt again. In fact, I wanted to burn every maternity outfit I had, but I literally had nothing else that fit.

Eventually, my breasts deflated. The bleeding ceased. Some of my old pants fit again. Big baggy sweaters covered a lumpy midsection. And eventually, I stopped hating my body enough to give it some care. I eased my aching body onto the floor and did some gentle stretches. I got a massage (my husband made the appointment for me and explained the situation so the massage therapist was not alarmed when I cried during it). I began to feel that, rather than betraying me, my body and I had both been sucker punched and we were now trying to recover together from the shock. I was also motivated to take care of my body, because I was certain—even in the depths of my despair—that I wanted to have another baby. I knew it would never make up for what we had lost, but loving Eliza had shown me how much I wanted to have a baby that I got to bring home.

CHAPTER 6

At first, I was too depleted to be angry. Anger was futile because I had nowhere to direct my rage. I felt empty and exhausted from the weight of my grief. Later, even though there was no one to blame for her loss and, as far as we knew, no way it could have been prevented, I became furious that *my* baby was dead. Why *me*? Why *my* baby girl? I knew loss was random and arbitrary, but I was angry that the odds had not been in my favor. It was so senseless.

These flashes of anger relieved the monotony of sadness. I found myself furious with other parents who didn't fully appreciate the gift they had been given. I hated anyone who joked that they were giving away a misbehaving child. I was breathless with fury when I saw someone at a gas station with a toddler without a car seat, blatantly endangering the child. My entire face felt hot with rage when a pregnant friend told me that she was opting out of the extra monitoring her doctor had recommended because "it was such a pain to schedule." I was beyond angry when I heard about parents disowning LGBTQ teens, and stories of child abuse made me apoplectic. I knew the world was colossally unfair, but the injustices were overwhelming and I burned with outrage. Didn't these people know how lucky they are? Didn't they realize how precarious the lives of children are?

I was also angry in a specific way with the woman who taught my Bradley method birthing classes. I was angry that after all the reading and studying I'd done for class, my labor and delivery experience was nothing like she had said it would be. She'd emphasized stages of labor and how we could track our labor progress by paying attention to particular sensations, but that had not been my experience at all, even before I found out Eliza's heart was no longer beating. I was angry that she considered the worst-case scenario to be "unnecessary interventions" resulting in a C-section. She had made me feel like I had control of everything as long as I stayed calm and focused during labor and avoided Pitocin. Instead, I had lost control of my entire life and even though I followed all her instructions to the letter, I had a dead baby.

If I ever were to teach a birthing class (which of course I never, ever, ever will) I would start the class by saying, "I don't want to scare or worry anyone unnecessarily, but I want to acknowledge the reality that 1 in 160 births end with heartbreak and tragedy, for reasons that are sometimes unexplained. It is unlikely that this will happen to you, but it is possible that your life or the life of someone you know will be directly or indirectly affected by stillbirth at some point. These tragedies are largely unpredictable and unpreventable. Please understand that what you are doing right now is an act of love for your baby, and just by being here, you are doing the best you can to protect and care for your baby. Should you find yourself coping with an unexpected loss, please know that I will do my best to provide support and resources for you."

My instructor said and did nothing of the kind. She emphasized to all of us that excessive monitoring would lead to a "cascade of interventions." She didn't ever mention that those interventions could be potentially life-saving for a baby in distress. She suggested that we wanted to avoid monitoring and excessive ultrasounds, implying that such measures could be potentially harmful instead of explaining that sometimes they are necessary and critical for prenatal care.

I was also angry with her because when Eliza died a few weeks before her due date, we were barely halfway through the course we'd paid hundreds of dollars for and she didn't offer us a refund. (The doula we had hired but never called quickly mailed a sympathy card and returned the deposit we'd made for her services after I emailed her our sad news, which I thought was so kind.) I was angry because this instructor had stressed the necessity of eating 100 grams of protein a day—an enormous amount that was far more than I usually got, eating a reasonably healthy vegetarian diet. Still, I tried valiantly to reach that number, eating eggs and cheese like it was my job. And yet, it didn't save my baby. At my six-week follow-up appointment, I asked my doctor in tears if maybe Eliza didn't get enough protein? He was incredulous that this was even a concern, and did all he could to ease my concerns about that.

Now, I think some of my anger was warranted. In retrospect, and with the benefit of the passage of time and subsequent experiences with pregnancy, I find that her messages were well-intentioned but at times inappropriate, misguided, and even incorrect. Some of my anger was misplaced: I was angry with this instructor because I had trusted her to prepare me, to tell me what to expect and instead I was completely blindsided by the death of my baby.

Even at the time, I knew that not all my anger with her was fair, but I also knew that her response to us was not compassionate. After all, we thwarted her message about the benefit of "natural birth" and hands-off prenatal care. What upset me was that, while some of what she said was true—sometimes monitoring alerts us to concerns that turn out to be nothing and sometimes there are unnecessary interventions during labor and delivery—but she should have qualified those statements by acknowledging that in the big picture, a living child is the ultimate goal. She should have clarified her statements so that it didn't sound like parents who *did* need to seek a different kind of medical care during pregnancy were endangering their baby by doing so.

I emailed her to tell her what happened, to explain why we wouldn't be attending any more classes. She called me and I told her the story of Eliza's birth. She assured me that her death wasn't my fault, but I wasn't convinced. She made it a point to ask that we return the books we'd borrowed from her. She promised that she'd check back in with us soon.

She sent an email to everyone in the class—including us, as we were still in the group listserv—to tell them what had happened. She ended the email by telling everyone that I'd had an un-medicated birth and if I could do it under "those circumstances," they could certainly do it, too. We asked to be removed from the mailing list.

She failed to remove us after our request, so we got an update when another couple in the class had a (healthy, living) baby. David made a second request and she removed my email, but not his. He got another update—this time a couple had a healthy homebirth! When he told me he was still getting her emails, I sent a strongly worded request that she remove his email from her list and not contact us further. I dropped the borrowed books through a mail slot on my way to a therapy appointment. I wrote an angry letter of complaint to the official Bradley method website, but I'm not sure I ever sent it. I never heard from her again.

I was also furious that the hospital sent us a bill. Obviously, we'd used their services, and naturally we were charged for that, but it still made me angry. It seemed so unfair that we owed an enormous amount of money after our baby died. Logically, I understood it. Emotionally, I railed against it. I called to set up a payment plan, my voice thick with unshed tears.

I knew other bereaved parents who had good and specific reasons to be angry with a medical provider or a health care system that had failed them, and that is anger on an entirely different level. It would have been different, I'm sure, if someone in particular was at fault, but there was no one to blame for this—which left only me. And if her death wasn't my fault, then I was mad at myself for assuming that my healthy and normal pregnancy guaranteed me a healthy baby to bring home.

My anger would grow and dissolve and twist and redirect itself in the months to come. It was usually an impotent rage, left unexpressed, me shaking my fist at the universe. I was angry with God, with the medical establishment's limited research on stillbirth, with every pregnant mother who assumed their baby would be fine (which was basically all of them), with every well-meaning person who dared utter a sentence beginning with the phrase "At least...", with the inconsiderate driver who cut me off in traffic, with the parenting magazine that kept showing up in my mailbox, and I was also pretty pissed off at that prenatal yoga instructor with the soothing voice who had made me feel like showing up on Monday nights to do cat-cow stretches at the YMCA was one way to keep my baby safe and healthy. *How dare she let me assume my baby would live?*

Anger bubbled up and then settled like icy rocks in my stomach when the cards I sent out to commemorate Eliza's first birthday were met with total silence from my husband's side of the family, and I sent emails filled with righteous outrage to his relatives whom I felt had failed us. I realize now that they were also grieving in their own way, and that they had no idea how to process our grief. (But really. Anything but silence would have been fine.)

My friend Sarah got a set of garage sale dishes after her son Otis died. They were intended as an outlet for her rage—so she could throw them and break them and hear them smash and shatter. She loved the gesture, but when I talked to her about them, she hadn't broken the dishes yet. They were still sitting in the cardboard box in the garage, waiting for the right moment. I wondered, as I talked to her, when that moment would come.

For a minute, there, I craved my own box of smash-dishes, but then I wondered if I would ever throw them. It's not that I wasn't angry enough. It's just that the world already felt so sharp and messy, I wasn't sure it needed more broken things.

When I look back now, I think that my fury burned white hot and then was quickly dampened by my tears. It wasn't that I wasn't angry—it's that I didn't have the energy to sustain it. My anger had nowhere to go. As angry as I felt, my fury fizzled quickly under the soggy weight of sadness. Rage was a brief respite from the heavy, suffocating fog of sorrow. No matter how furious I was with the world at large or with that one pregnant woman in my neighborhood who kept walking by my house, there was no action I could take, no tantrum I could throw, that would bring my baby back to me.

PART THREE

THINGS FALL APART

CHAPTER 7

When I returned from the hospital, I felt lost in my own two-bedroom house. My home hadn't changed—the Christmas tree was still sparkling in the living room, my school bag was still sitting in the corner of the dining room, my maternity clothes still hanging in the closet—but I was a completely different person. I walked in the front door and went straight to my bedroom, hoping to sleep away this bad dream I was living. I lay on the bed, curled and tucked into the fetal position, clutching a blanket that had been wrapped around Eliza in the hospital. It was yellow, the color of baby ducks, crocheted, the yarn too scratchy for a newborn. It had probably been looped and knotted with love and empathy before it had covered my Baby Duck for a few photographs. I hated that blanket, the memory of her dead body so still beneath it. I loved that blanket for having touched her, for being a tangible thing that connected me to her. I twisted the crocheted loops around my fingers until they throbbed from lack of circulation.

We had two small dogs—a friendly, snuggly pug/beagle mix named Cooper, and a temperamental, tiny and occasionally vicious Pekingese/poodle mix named Little Mac. The dogs were thrilled to see us return from the hospital. I could hardly believe we'd been away only overnight.

Little Mac, the pek-a-poo, was in her elder years, and she'd never been snuggly or affectionate even though she was a perfect lap-size. We had learned to adapt to her lack of social skills, and I found her endearing in her own bizarre way. All physical affection had to be initiated by her—attempt to pet her without invitation and she was likely to snap and bite. David and I had had countless conversations about how Little Mac would adjust to the baby, and what we would do if the adjustment didn't go well. I'd cried when I imagined having to re-home Little Mac and hoped that she would adjust to having a baby in the house. I loved her, but I wasn't sure who else would be willing to adopt a cranky old dog with a tendency to be violent who was disinclined to pee outside in inclement weather.

Little Mac had her own dog bed in nearly every room of the house because she wasn't cuddly. Her sight and hearing were degenerating, so she preferred to be in a position where she could view the room but feel safe and tucked away. She rarely joined us on the couch anymore because it was getting harder for her to jump up and she had never enjoyed snuggling even when she was active and spry.

But as I lay on my bed that morning, staring blankly

at the wall, gripping that crocheted baby blanket as though it were a lifeline and wondering how in the hell I would ever manage to live this life in a fog of misery, I felt the mattress shift ever so slightly as 12 pounds of elderly dog leapt up next to me. I turned to look, and that unpredictable, temperamental little dog who hadn't been on my lap for months, nuzzled her head gently against me, stepped over my legs, then curled up in the hollow of my stomach and sighed.

They say dogs can sense grief—a shift in body language, perhaps even a scent. Whatever possessed her to hop up on my bed that day, it was perhaps the only comfort that anyone could have offered me in that moment that I could have accepted fully. This was a grief too deep for words, too big for condolences. Little Mac was there to abide with me, to offer me all she could in the small comfort of her warm little body next to mine.

As the days went on, when I was still too raw or too tired for human contact, for the pressure of conversation and reporting on how I was doing, the silent companionship of my dogs offered me something intangible but necessary. Little Mac was never so snuggly again, but Cooper made up for it with his eagerness to be right next to me and his gentle snoring. They expected next to nothing from me—food, water, and a walk, if I was up to it—and in return they would abide with me in my pain. The warm bodies and beating hearts of my dogs kept me tethered to a world where they made me feel wanted and needed, even though what I wanted most was no longer there.

My dogs' response to me—a quiet closeness, lack of judgment, contentment just to be near me—was the gift that we humans struggle to give each other. We should all be so lucky as to be loved by a dog. They could not right the greatest wrong of my life, but unlike so many humans who flail in the face of tragedy or move instinctively away from those who are suffering, my dogs were more than willing to sit with me in it. It was all they could do, and it was enough.

CHAPTER 8

Waking in the morning was the process of becoming aware of the heavy pit in my stomach. Aside from the permanently knotted and nauseating weight in the center of my guts, there was nothing but emptiness where once my life had been brimming with anticipation and activity. In the weeks leading up to Eliza's birth, I felt so full. Yes—my stomach and breasts were enormous, but my whole life felt full. My house was full of baby gear. My bag was full of end-of-semester grading to get through. My calendar was chock-full of parties and meet ups as the semester ended and we were moving toward the holidays. I wanted one more coffee date with this friend, one more dinner with that couple, one more errand to squeeze in before taking a break over the holidays. My heart was full of gratitude and excitement as we looked forward to meeting this baby shortly after Christmas.

Then, before my semester officially ended or the holiday season got into its full swing, I left the hospital completely empty with nothing to look forward to.

Deflated, depleted. My stomach still looked alarmingly puffy, but I was an empty shell of myself.

This emptiness was frightening. This was the emptiness that pulled me toward the edge of a big abyss, promising an escape from the blankness of my life, if only I had the stomach for it and could stand the idea of hurting everyone I loved (while they were already grieving).

(I did not have the stomach nor the energy for it, and I could not stand the idea of causing further pain, which is why I assured my therapist I did not have suicidal thoughts. The truth is that I had no intention of acting on them, but like almost every mother I know who has lost a child, those thoughts flickered around the sharpest edges of my grief.)

I couldn't see how my emptiness would ever fill. Nothing—no one—could ever take Eliza's place, and the hole she left in my life was so vast, so gaping. I felt like a ghost town, haunted by the baby I thought I would have, the mother I thought I would be, the life I thought I would live. In place of those things that had once felt like certainties, I had only vacancies. I was emptiness and ruin.

I couldn't see my way out. I could only take the tiniest step forward and do the next thing that needed to be done. Each day was long and excruciatingly empty. Weeks and months went by before the emptiness started to fill. The substitutes for Eliza were poor. I wanted to be busy caring for a newborn. I didn't want a spring break vacation, coffee dates with friends, or endless hours to binge-watch television. I didn't want another broken-hearted trudge around the neighborhood with my dogs.

To lose a baby is to feel your entire life drain away with her. To go from near-bursting with love, anticipation, and a squirmy, kicky baby in the belly to hunched, hollow, and empty-handed, staring into a blank future as your wheelchair rolls toward an elevator. It's the kind of emptiness vacuum that sucks out all the air in the room. It's the sort of vacancy that makes it impossible to care about anything else other than the raw and gaping blank space in your heart, in your arms, in your life—that space that was supposed to be filled with your baby and instead is aching with emptiness.

An empty nursery. Empty baby shoes. Empty bouncer. Empty swing. Empty crib. The ache I felt around that emptiness was as though the dearest thing to my heart had been ripped out from my body and taken from me, never to be returned. As, of course, it had been.

I did not know in those early, empty days, if my life would ever feel full again. I did not know how much time it would take. I did not know how the gaping pit of grief would shrink a little, the edges get less raw and dangerous, as relationships and a renewed sense of purpose would eventually create a fence and a safety net for me. For a long time, I only knew what it felt like to feel empty.

In the face of that emptiness, and the ugly rawness of my early grief, I had friends who stepped back. They were sad for me, but they were also mourning the loss of the person I had been in their life. I missed the person I had been, too, but I didn't have enough space in my grief yet to be sad about that, or to acknowledge their grief. Friendship with me was no longer a mutual relationship or a two-way street. I had nothing to give.

Fortunately, I also had friends who stepped up with insistent kindness. They showed up at my house with DVDs of *Anne of Green Gables* and the early seasons of *Grey's Anatomy*. They brought sandwiches and dropped off cheese and crackers to tempt my appetite. They knocked on the door and didn't blink when I opened it grudgingly, bleary-eyed, with unbrushed hair, wearing David's college t-shirts and boxer shorts. They defined what it is to abide with someone, gently filling in the emptiness with their presence, not asking for much of anything in return. Checking in with texts day after day, even when I could hardly bring myself to reply. If friendship is about give and take, these women understood instinctively that I had nothing to give, and they were willing to sit in that imbalance as long as it took for me to regain my footing. Some of them I'm still in touch with today, and others have moved more to the periphery of my contacts, but I will never forget the lifeline they provided.

CHAPTER 9

"They say these things happen for a reason," one woman I'm acquainted with said to me a few months after Eliza's death.

She was trying to be kind. In that moment, I wanted to murder her. Let her figure out my reason.

My face got hot, blood pounded in my ears. What I said in response was, "We did all kinds of testing. They couldn't find a reason."

But even if we'd had a clear answer, even if there were a chromosomal issue, or a genetic anomaly, or a completely unpredictable and incurable problem with the baby's development, that reason would not have made a difference. I still wanted my baby no matter what. I felt like this woman was implying that something must have been wrong with my baby, as though that information would have made it easier to cope with her death. Perhaps she meant to say that there was probably no way Eliza could have been saved, but to me it sounded as though she was saying my baby was better off dead than imperfect in some way.

On the one hand, certainly, there must have been some biological *reason* that Eliza's heart stopped beating (Or random chance? A misfire of the universe?). On the other hand, there is no *reason* that a child should die. A clear explanation was not within our reach. This confusion tormented me. If we didn't know what happened, how could we prevent it from happening again?

I wanted desperately to know that it wasn't my fault, that there wasn't some way it could have been prevented if I'd just paid more attention, done more kick counting, not eaten something, not missed those prenatal vitamins that one weekend we went out of town. I wondered, too, how I would feel if we had discovered I had an unknown genetic issue, something we hadn't tested for because I appeared to be young and healthy. How would blame sit with me then? There was some relief that we didn't have evidence that it *was* my fault, but at the same time, I was baffled and unsure how we would move forward without answers.

I attended a grief support meeting where I told Eliza's story. I concluded by saying, "And the worst part is that we don't have any answers or explanations for what happened."

I don't know why I said that. That was not the worst part. The worst part was that my daughter was dead. But also, I couldn't stop obsessing over *why* I couldn't have prevented it.

Another bereaved mother at the meeting spoke up

gently but firmly. "We know why my daughter died," she said, having told the story of her baby's chromosomal abnormality, her voice soft and thick with unshed tears. "It doesn't really help to have answers."

Whether or not we ever got a reason for her death, there could be no satisfactory answer for why a baby dies before she is born. There could never be a good enough "reason," even if we have a medical explanation.

It is a reversal of the natural order. It is the completely wrong ending tacked on to a story we thought we could predict. We're left bewildered. We thought we knew exactly what to expect—a baby—and we stare, shocked and confused, into a completely different future.

Joseph Conrad gets credit for a quote that says, "We must let go of the life we have planned to accept the one we have waiting for us." This sounds like good advice, but it's incredibly difficult when the last thing we want to let go of is the child around whom we have planned our entire life. If I wasn't walking a path that led me to Eliza, I had no idea where I was going. Life had been clear and focused—like a love tunnel that led me to my baby girl. Now I was off course and totally lost. No other plan could ever measure up to the future we had dreamed for our baby girl, and suddenly we were stuck figuring out how to improvise this new life and how to move forward on this path we never wanted to walk.

CHAPTER 10

I lost countless hours of sleep pondering whether there was a reason for Eliza's death. Is it possible that *everything happens for a reason*? I've heard people say it. I've read it on rustic signs hung up in bathrooms. I've said it myself when trying to offer encouragement and not knowing what to say: "Everything happens for a reason." Before Eliza died, I was one of those people who probably would have agreed with this statement, but I had never considered fully what it meant.

I understand the desire to organize life experiences following a narrative that makes logical sense even if we can't understand it in the moment. I understand that there are those whose faith enables them to think there is a greater plan we cannot see, but I do not think the faithful are required to believe that there is a reason babies die. I cannot begin to fathom the sort of reason that would ever feel like an acceptable excuse for her death—for me to learn a lesson? To be more compassionate? So that her sisters could be born? I reject those explanations.

My daughter was not a sacrificial lamb; I did not need an exercise in empathy or a guardian angel. There is no reason for her not to be here with us, except there was a terrible, random event that caused her death.

It's easy to explain a near-miss, a close-shave, a narrowly-avoided accident, a remarkable survival, by attributing it to the hand of fate/God. God must have been watching over that guy who walked away from a terrible car accident. We hear that sort of thing all the time.

But does that mean that God got careless or busy and that's why another car accident took out an entire family? Or that the lack of divine intervention means that it was God's plan for innocent people to be cut down in the prime of their lives? Was there a "reason" for that? It was their time?

The fact is, we devise methods to intervene and save lives all the time. That's not thwarting a master plan. That's being reasonable and responsible and pro-active. Why would anyone want to believe that we are passive creatures, pawns of fate? And yet I hear this line of thinking all the time.

It's easy to believe that things happen for a reason when everything in your life has worked out well so far, when the stakes have been relatively low. Let's assume there was a reason I didn't make the team. Let's assume there was a reason that the job offer went to someone else. Let's assume there was a reason my college boyfriend said that he thought we should not make post-gradua-tion plans together. I want to hold on to the idea that those disappointments happened so that I had space for better things to come into my life. This allows me to remain optimistic and open-minded about what comes next. But maybe there was no reason for any of those things—except my jumps weren't high enough, someone else was better qualified, and I had not yet refined my taste in boyfriends.

Before Eliza died, I was a pretty lucky girl. I liked to think there was a reason that my husband had moved to my hometown (obviously, to meet me). I liked to believe there was a reason that a random housing assignment in college had allowed me to make some of my best friends. My life was easy and comfortable, so it was easy and comfortable to believe that the people in my life came into it for a reason. There was a reason that I was supposed to move to this city, meet this friend, take this job, get introduced to these people. It was all part of a greater plan.

Now I think about all of this differently. Good things happened to me because I was privileged, I was lucky, and I worked hard to make the most of what I had.

You see, if I believed that those good things happened for a greater reason, like my destiny, then I'd also have to believe that there is a reason that second graders get leukemia. I'd have to say that there's some reason that a tornado would crush a home and kill a family. There's a reason that an entire airplane full of innocent people was flown into an office building. There must be a reason that a drunk driver plowed into a young father on his way home from work. There's a reason that an electrical fire took the lives of two little girls.

And what could that reason be? How could anything possibly justify those tragedies? What kind of reasonable explanation could I ever be offered that would satisfactorily explain why my baby died?

Saying that everything happens for a reason implies that there will be compensation for our loss, when the fact is that there is nothing that will ever make up for it. It also suggests that those affected by a tragedy are expected to emerge on the other side, better, wiser, more appreciative. If your experience makes you bitter, angry, or chronically depressed, then we don't say those outcomes happened for a reason. We quietly think that perhaps you have not sufficiently learned your lesson.

Suggesting everything happens for a reason can also speak to the belief that the experiences of our life are divinely ordained. As someone who believes human beings have free will, I do not subscribe to this notion, although I appreciate the desire to think that everything is part of a mysterious plan. It's easy to say that when we are safely outside trauma and loss, or when we're trying desperately to make sense of it and random chaos is too frightening to consider. It would be nice to feel like our lives have a clear purpose and we can sit back and wait for that plan to unfold. Not to worry! It will all work out in the end! That is comforting for some, who get their happy ending. It is devastating for those whose outcomes are unfair or heartbreaking through no fault of their own. It also suggests that God parents through cruelty—like abusing kids who don't want to eat their vegetables. It ignores the most essential aspect of free will, which is that

God doesn't control what happens to us. I do not believe that God chooses for some babies to die, or that there is some pattern or lesson in that fate. But there is comfort in the notion of God being there with those who grieve, comfort in knowing that we can still shape a meaningful life out of our sorrow.

The only reason that terrible things happened, it seemed to me, was because as a caveat of having personal agency and free will, we must navigate a world in which random suffering (and sometimes deliberate cruelty) is a part of the human experience. This leads me to believe that it is also our moral imperative to do our part to alleviate the suffering of others. Instead of trying to figure out the reason for Eliza's death, I needed to find a reason to keep going.

I have come to believe that we seek spiritual and human connections because we need strength and community to face the random chaos of our reality, regardless of how we use faith to understand this world. Terrible things can, do, and will happen to us in this life, no matter what we believe, so we seek the grace to get through it and we try to help each other. I am not a theologian, but my understanding is that this perspective is not incompatible with any of the major religions in our world.

It does not mean that our lives are meaningless. Far from it. It means that we are called upon to shape meaning out of our lives. Everything happens for a reason, because we learn and grow from our experiences, not because a greater being is inflicting them upon us. Those of us who are religious may grow closer to God; others find themselves drifting away from their faith. While I could never be satisfied with the idea that my daughter died for some large reason, I do want to make her brief, beautiful life continue to have meaning in my own. I want the experience of being Eliza's mom to continue to shape me, just as my other most significant life experiences have done.

Substitute teaching at an elementary school became meaningful because I met my husband there. Eliza's birthday coming near the holidays becomes meaningful because we have collected many Christmas ornaments that make us think of her. We make a choice to give Eliza's death meaning when we honor her memory by doing good in her name.

But I don't think my baby died for a reason because I don't think there is a reason good enough to compensate for the death of a child. On a good day, our loss is a deeply meaningful part of our overall story. Other days, it's an impossibly messed up thing that happened to us and could have happened to anyone. There's no greater lesson here, no existential reason for this twist of fate. The death of a baby is not a teaching moment. It's a tragedy.

CHAPTER 11

As time went by and the emotions of anger, sorrow, and shame became more familiar, if not tolerable, I started to recognize additional things that had been lost—collateral damages. I found myself mourning these smaller losses, and the way they added up to a complete restructuring of my life. Nothing mattered as much as the loss of my baby, but these other, smaller losses were additional griefs, and they highlighted the way Eliza's death had shattered so much of my everyday experience.

One was the Greek restaurant in our neighborhood where we'd gotten in the habit of going every Friday for happy hour. I'd order a club soda and the hummus. The owners of the restaurant were a couple, and the woman was also pregnant and due around the same time I was, so towards the end of my pregnancy, it became a kind of joke to see if we'd both be waddling in on Friday.

I loved that place. It was the first restaurant where we'd been regulars, and I felt like I'd carved a little piece of home in a big city when David and I walked in and the bartender greeted us. The food was good; the happy hour specials were cheap. I enjoyed daydreaming about the wine list that I'd try after the baby came. It was nice to have a standing date with my husband and it was easy to imagine coming back in with the baby in the spring, eventually sitting out on the patio with a toddler. It felt like our place.

Then my baby died and we never went back. At first, we avoided it because I didn't want to leave the house to go anywhere at all. Then I didn't want to have to explain our loss. Then it was because the contrast between the hope I'd felt the last time I was there and the grief I was feeling now was too painful. Eventually, it felt like it had been too long. It was likely they wouldn't even remember us, but it wasn't our place anymore. I wasn't the person I'd been when I went there, and I didn't know how to get back to her.

This is a small thing in the grand scheme of it all, but it is a loss. It's one more thing that was destroyed when our plans dissolved into profound disappointment, when the comfortable familiarity of what we could expect from life transformed into a gaping unknown. I didn't miss that restaurant like I missed Eliza. It was a small and separate grief, a kind of poignant, nostalgic sadness—the same way I might have felt if the restaurant had closed or we'd moved to another city. It was like that restaurant and everything it had been for us was now lost to me forever, and I mourned that small loss of an enjoyable place to go on Fridays and the big loss of the entire Other Life it represented.

In fact, these secondary losses began adding up quickly, and while none of them was as brutal as losing Eliza, each one hurt in its own way.

My friends went ahead and gathered for a Christmas party that we'd all been planning since early November. It took place a week after we lost Eliza. Of course, we were still invited, but I had no desire to go. Logically, I knew there was no reason for them to cancel. It was a rare opportunity for our group to get together, a night reserved on everyone's calendars in a busy season. Our friends encouraged us to come, understood that we could not. I know they grieved with us, but they also got together and enjoyed themselves in a way in which we no longer felt capable. That felt like another loss. I was missing out not only on the party, but on all the ways my life would have naturally unfolded with Eliza here.

My friend Jamie and I used to talk or text daily. Literally not a day went by when we didn't check in with each other. She had a baby boy three months before I lost Eliza, and after Eliza died, I suddenly couldn't think of a thing to say to her. We talked a few times, but I starting letting her calls go to voicemail. Even though I was the one making the choice not to answer my phone, those daily conversations were a loss that I grieved as well. I wanted to be capable of having them. I grieved the change in our friendship, the loss of the person I used to be, my enjoyment of superficial chitchat, my ability to reach out and share in other people's everyday pleasures and challenges. We'd been pregnant together and looked forward to our life and our families changing in the same way at the same time. Then my life veered off course, and I lost that easy connection with her.

I had expected to be nine months pregnant for Christmas of 2010. I had planned to spend that holiday break in between semesters putting the finishing touches on the nursery, washing loads of tiny pink pajamas, and reveling in Christmas traditions that we'd be sharing with a little one the next time the season came around. We'd already started having so many conversations that began with, "Next year, we'll…" After Eliza died, I refused to celebrate Christmas at all. There would be no church, no gift opening, no big dinner. I did not want to acknowledge the holiday at all. This was my choice, and it was the only decision that felt right at the time—going through the motions of the holiday would have been incredibly painful for me—but I still grieved the loss of the holiday that I'd already planned and looked forward to. Because Eliza's birthday was early December, I assumed that Christmas would always be a heavy season of grief for me, a favorite time of year forever marred by grief and loss. I grieved because I felt like every Christmas for the rest of my life would be overshadowed by her loss.

(I didn't realize at the time that it would be a heavy season of grief for me, and still capable of holding on to its holiday magic. I didn't yet understand that those things could coexist.)

I grieved all the ways I had changed, both superficially and profoundly. I wanted to be funny, lighthearted, quick to laugh. I did not think I could ever be those things again. As a result, I often felt awkward and isolated, even when surrounded by friends. I didn't know how to be myself because I didn't recognize the person I had become in this role of bereaved mother. I didn't want to be depressed and crying all the time, but I also couldn't bear to act differently than I felt. And even if I was having a relatively good day, I hated the idea that my friends might think that I'd somehow reconciled myself to Eliza's death.

I found myself making all kinds of small changes in my daily routines, letting go of things that had once seemed simple or easy. I changed the paths I took around the city to avoid driving by the hospital or my favorite children's clothing boutique. I canceled literally every plan I'd made for the foreseeable future. I quit watching my favorite TV show because of a pregnancy plot line. These were small and relatively unimportant compared to the loss of my daughter, but they were losses that hurt, too. And sometimes they meant that I was also hurting or disappointing people I loved when I couldn't show up for their housewarming party or their child's birthday party.

For a while, my grief made it impossible for me to maintain relationships, to be generous and supportive, to be the kind of friend or family member I had always tried to be. I had always put together a family photo calendar for my husband's grandmother for Christmas. I could no longer bear to spend my time arranging collages of cousins and nieces and nephews celebrating milestones my child would never reach. My grief made me feel selfish, but it came out of a necessity for self-preservation.

Those who could wait it out—and I am so fortunate to say that was the clear majority of my friends and family members—were still there when I could forge more equitable relationships with them again. But there were some bridges burned, some fissures irreparable. Collateral damage. This is the additional cost of grief.

Sometimes collateral damage looks like a career path that is no longer tenable, or a volunteer position you can no longer return to. Sometimes friendships cannot survive the tempest of grief. There are marriages that crumble under the relentless stress of this level of sorrow (although, in my anecdotal experience, the relationships that end after losing a child rarely end because of grief—either grief brings to focus other incompatibilities, or they emerge later, unrelated to the shared loss). Collateral damage is usually smaller and hardly seems worth being sad about, except it's so many small things. It might be a tradition you once held dear but that now makes you cry. It might be a food you craved during pregnancy and now can't eat without the taste of bitterness on your tongue. It might be a hobby or a habit or place that has been forever altered, something that you can't revisit or that you now desperately want to avoid.

I have learned—the hard way—that *altered* does not necessarily mean *ruined*. But it does mean different. And change of any sort is an additional loss—even if you are the one making the decision to avoid that person, place, or thing. I can enjoy hummus and pita bread now—but I still haven't been back to that restaurant. I have reconnected with friends, but our relationships have shifted with the passage of time and changes in circumstances. I can see pictures of my niece and nephew without seeing them as markers of what Eliza will never experience but I'll never look at our family photo calendar without a twinge in my heart for the little girl whose smiling face is not included among its pages.

We have to make space to grieve collateral losses alongside and separately from grieving our children. Those losses are also real, difficult, and painful, even if they also seem minor in comparison. The only way I have found to make up for collateral losses is to begin to accept collateral gains. The recompense for the loss of a child will never be adequate, but in avoiding places I'd gone regularly when I was pregnant, I found a new coffee shop that allowed me to hide out in a corner booth, where the barista pretended not to notice that I always looked like I'd been crying (because I always had been) and I eventually began meeting up with a friend there. My Friday night happy hour shifted into a Wednesday night grief support group, but in that shift I found a new circle of friends who were walking their own journeys of loss. David and I created a new date night tradition of Chinese takeout and *Survivor*, which is blessedly reliable for never having a pregnancy plotline. These were a slow build, a long time coming after the sweeping and instantaneous devastation of losing our daughter. I mourned all the parts of me that seemed to die along with her. Collateral gains softened some of the losses, but it was still hard and messy to make those adjustments when even the simplest decisions felt loaded.

CHAPTER 12

After Eliza died, I was afraid of everything. In the novel *Mrs. Dalloway*, Virginia Woolf writes of her title character, "It seemed to her very, very dangerous to live even one day." This was how I felt after Eliza died. No longer was the world an inviting and delightful place. It had been luck and privilege that let me see it that way, and my luck had run out. Now, I saw the world as it really was: fraught with danger and laced with accidents waiting to happen. I was afraid of everything after Eliza's death. Previously, I'd held countless superficial fears—of not measuring up to someone else's expectations, of missing out on a social event, of embarrassing myself publicly. These faded away, revealed as meaningless in the face of actual loss and pain. But real fears—of death, of further loss, of loneliness—were amplified and multiplied. I was bereft without my daughter, but I still had people I loved. And every day I was afraid of losing them.

I feared my husband dying in a car accident. I feared my parents dying in a car accident as they drove across the state to visit us. My brother was living in South Korea at the time. We had visited the summer that my pregnancy was just starting to become visible, and I was nervous about taking my bump overseas. I had made sure to get my doctor's okay before traveling internationally, and I had purchased a couple of souvenirs for Eliza, already looking forward to telling her about the time she traveled to South Korea when she was still in my belly. Now, I kept thinking of my brother dying on another continent, victim of a North Korean weapons test, or maybe hit by one of those scooters that drive alarmingly fast on the sidewalk.

Part of me knew that these concerns verged on the irrational, but both my heart and my head were running at a low throttle of panic because I knew from firsthand experience that life was incredibly fragile, so easily lost, able to slip away if I wasn't vigilant. When my husband would arrive home from work, I'd greet him at the door and, inevitably, when he hugged me, I'd burst into tears. Tears of relief that he had made it home. Tears of exhaustion from the effort of *not* crying all day long. Tears of anxiety that this might be the last time he arrived home safely.

A few weeks after Eliza died, I had a nightmare that my dog was run over by a bicycle, that the tire split him up the middle. I crouched in the street screaming and trying to hold his gray-pink intestines in his body. My brain kept forcing forward this newly-realized awareness of how delicate our bodies are, how easily harmed, how irreparable the damage that could be inflicted.

We know on an intellectual level of course that we are vulnerable. A stray bullet, a covert tumor, a drunk driver veering across a few inches of paint... we can be taken out at any moment without warning. As humans, we recognize this truth and then we promptly ignore it so that we can live our lives. But now, having experienced death where I was counting on finding a new life, I found it impossible to ignore the constant, looming threat of mortality everywhere.

If a baby who seemed healthy—who was growing at a regular rate, who was moving and grooving in my belly, whose heart had four chambers, whose umbilical cord had three blood vessels, whose mother was not a drug addict, did not have chronic health problems, was not malnourished or impoverished—if this baby could die in utero, then what was keeping any of the rest of us going?

Suddenly, my healthy, active, athletic husband seemed just as likely to die of a brain aneurysm as to survive the day. My heart would literally flutter, a slightly irregular heartbeat, and I wondered if this was it—a valve no longer functioning, a thirty-year-old woman dying of a heart attack.

No longer could I assume that the universe conspired to bring me success. Rather, the universe was fierce and indifferent, a neutral force perfectly willing to strip me of everything that mattered and everyone I loved. What did my personal disasters and small scale tragedies matter in the grand scheme of things? The universe was just as likely to kill anyone as let them live, or so it seemed.

I was constantly afraid of losing someone else I loved.

I was also afraid of learning to live without Eliza. I was afraid of my grief and pain lasting forever and afraid of what it would mean if it ceased. Hope and optimism had been replaced by fear and anxiety. To feel otherwise would be putting myself at risk for the world to dupe me yet again.

The only way to manage my fear of the future and heartache for the past was to practice sitting in the present—the mindfulness my therapist talked about, but which I resisted. I was afraid that being in the present moment would leave me unprepared for future calamity. If only I could anticipate every horror that might befall me, create a contingency plan for each possibility, then I might be able to avoid disaster.

Slowly, I came to accept that even if I could anticipate misfortune, I would not be able to avoid it. I began to acknowledge that predicting loss would not protect me from it. And I took my therapist's advice to count my breaths and sit in the moment when anxiety threatened to overwhelm me. I had been reluctant to return to yoga practice—after all, yoga didn't save my baby—but eventually I went to a restorative class, where we spent a great deal of effort wedging bolsters and blankets under various body parts so that we could lay in unexpectedly comfortable and supported positions and just breathe. The instructor would dim the lights and I would do my best to steady my breathing as hot tears ran down my temples and into my hair, sometimes trickling behind my ears, until I finally allowed my body to relax and I focused only on the inhale and exhale.

Yoga did not cure me. My fears remained. But, my resilience slowly grew. It didn't feel like strength as much as building my tolerance for pain. But perhaps those are not so different, after all.

CHAPTER 13

In the early days of grief, my pain felt so immense that I couldn't imagine it wouldn't be permanent. My daughter would always be dead, so I would always feel like this: desperate, brittle, frightened, jealous. I felt like Miss Havisham in *Great Expectations*. And that scared me.

When I taught Charles Dickens's *Great Expectations* the summer before I got pregnant with Eliza, I framed Miss Havisham as a villain. Or, I should say, I suggested to my students that the narrator frames her as a villain.

Miss Havisham is a woman who was jilted on her wedding day by a lover who turned out to have double-crossed her with the help of her brother. While this should make her sympathetic, in the aftermath of her heartbreak, she becomes angry, bitter, and hateful. She stops all the clocks at the time of her wedding, leaves the feast to rot on the table, and never removes her wedding dress, the aging lace falling to pieces around her. She apparently was wearing one shoe when she got word of the broken engagement, so she clomps around in one shredded wedding slipper, the other yellowing in its unworn condition on her bureau. She adopts a baby girl, Estella, and spoils her, but also raises her to have no understanding of love. She acts this way because she is utterly absorbed by her own pain.

In class, we discussed her as one of the "monsters" of the novel—an example of what a human being becomes when they allow themselves to get so caught up in their own pain that they come to enjoy inflicting pain on others. She is a warning of sorts, an exaggerated depiction of someone who lets disappointment poison their entire life and even blight the lives of the next generation.

Because she is so destructive, I never felt a lot of sympathy for Miss Havisham. Then my baby died, and with her went all my great expectations for my own future. I suddenly felt like I *was* Miss Havisham.

I mean, I wasn't limping around my house in one shoe and sagging maternity clothes with all the clocks stopped at the time of Eliza's death, but I sort of *wanted* to be. That scenario now made a strange kind of sense to me. It was such a devastating event—I wanted it permanently marked as such. I understood Miss Havisham in a way I had never expected. There's a reason why W. H. Auden's famous poem about grief begins with "Stop all the clocks." I, too, wanted to stop everything and refuse to move forward. I might as well wear the same clothes day after day, letting them slowly fall apart. I wanted to take the sympathy food and flowers that people had sent and leave them sitting on the table to rot and attract bugs. Who would care? Not me. I wanted to keep the shades drawn and the room dark. I wanted to refuse to see people. I wanted never to leave my house. I understood how her grief turned to bitterness and anger, how it poisoned her. I could feel my own sadness draining away my capacity to be happy for other people.

Resisting this urge to remain stuck in my grief took all the energy that I could muster—and a lot of therapy. I talked with my therapist about the possibility of medication, which I resisted because I felt that taking an antidepressant would mean that I was depressed instead of grieving an actual and specific loss. Although I managed to function without medication, I wish now that I had not been so adamantly opposed to it. I thought it would just mask my pain, but now I think it could have served as a crutch in the best sense of the word—a device intended to assist me in getting through the worst of it until I could manage on my own. But I worked closely with my therapist, without medication. I forced myself to shower. I wrestled my emotions into words, writing and journaling. I read. Mostly fiction with clear demarcations of good and evil and no plots involving babies or pregnancies (and no World War II fiction—the anxiety of losing control of my family's well-being was too much for me and I wanted books to feel like an escape). I made myself do laundry, I escaped into television, I occasionally looked at Eliza's pictures and cried. I cried for what I had lost in losing her, and I cried because I was still afraid I was losing myself.

I'd experienced sadness before—heartache, disappointment, grief—but never in a way that was overwhelming. I had never been so desperately sad. I had a vague notion that women who lost children also lost their minds. Surely that's why people said things like, "I can't even imagine." I'd seen grieving mothers depicted on television. They were checked into mental hospitals or abusing prescription drugs or kidnapping other people's kids.

I genuinely feared becoming a monster. And as sad and hopeless as I felt in those early days and weeks, I knew that I didn't want to become so overwhelmed by my own sadness that I ceased to function entirely—no matter how appealing that seemed in the short term.

But still. There were long, dark, desperate days in the early weeks after Eliza's death. I didn't want to leave the house by myself. I'd get dizzy standing in my kitchen and realize it was because I had forgotten to breathe. I might have gotten up and put on clean clothes every day, but I spent almost all day every day curled up on my couch, waiting for David to get home from work so I could curl up next to him.

My faculty mentor from grad school wrote me a letter expressing her condolences and told me she had a good friend who had lost her first child and went on to have a family and a full life. She assured me that Eliza's death was "a great sadness, but not a harbinger of things to come." I'm not sure anyone else spoke so specifically to my greatest fear—that with Eliza's death my life had veered off onto a path of death, grief, and darkness from which I would never escape. I wanted to take my professor at her word. I needed her condolences to be promises.

Eventually, the desperation, the weight, the urgency of grief lifted. I can still recall that heaviness, though. And I understand Miss Havisham differently. The novel may depict her as a sort of monster, but I know what it is to experience a grief that makes you feel monstrous. Sometimes that feeling is justified. Sometimes being human with a broken heart is just too hard.

My experience of bereaved mothers now has little in common with the popular depiction of women who completely shut down and lose themselves to sorrow. Most of us don't, in fact, collapse forever under the weight of grief. We do not feel strong, but we gain strength by carrying the heavy burden of our sorrow and not sinking under it as we move forward in our lives. What we want most is what C.S. Lewis calls "[t]he happy past restored," but given that impossibility, what we discover is that we are, in fact, capable of moving into a future that holds space for both grief and joy. It just takes a lot of time and effort for us to get there.

CHAPTER 14

There's an Arab proverb that says, *Love sees sharply, hatred sees even more sharp, but jealousy sees the sharpest for it is love and hate at the same time.* I was overcome with jealously in the year following Eliza's death. Many of my close friends were pregnant or had recently had a baby. I felt love and resentment twisted up into a complicated emotional cocktail—feeling jealous of people I cared about, hating myself for being angry and unable to rise above my own loss. It wasn't that I wished my loss on anyone else—nothing could be further from the truth— but it still tore me up that my friends with whom I had shared so many life experiences now got to have what I didn't. They got to take for granted what had been ripped away from me. And if they weren't taking it for granted, then they were appreciating it even more, because they saw my loss and were glad it wasn't theirs.

When I was about halfway through my pregnancy with Eliza, we'd invited several of my friends from college over for a barbecue. There were six of us there who had lived together on campus, studied and partied together, graduated the same year, consoled each other through break-ups, been bridesmaids in each other's weddings, and discussed paint colors for each other's first houses. We had literally been taking photos together since we were eighteen and in the same dorm, and this night was no exception—we all lined up to take a photo together. Four of us—including me—were visibly pregnant. The two who weren't pregnant had babies about a year old. As we wrapped our arms around each other and beamed at our husbands holding cell phones and snapping photos, I thought about the random beauty of a college dorm rooming assignment and the fact that we were now entering another season of life together.

Before Eliza died, it was so easy to imagine a future of backyard barbecues and Friday night pizza parties, the kids running wild, the parents having a few drinks. Everything in my life felt like it was right on schedule and I was entering the next stage of life with my friends alongside me, as we'd always done. It gave me a false sense of control and achievement, allowing me to assume that if I worked hard and made responsible decisions, things would continue to work out in my favor.

That photo of us was taken in August. My friend Jamie had her baby boy in October. I visited her at the hospital and cradled him on top of my pregnant belly, counting down the three months to my due date.

In November, my friend Stephanie had twins. I sent her a pair of onesies that said "Cookies" and "Milk." We were so happy that they were healthy and her recovery was smooth.

A week later I had Eliza, and she never took a breath.

A couple of weeks after Eliza was born, my friend Carolina had her baby boy on Christmas day. Another friend left me a voicemail to let me know that Carolina and her son were doing well.

Then it was New Year's Eve. My daughter had been dead for three weeks. My friends all had healthy, perfect babies. They were all moving forward together, as we had planned, but I had taken this sharp and unexpected detour. Their road was well-paved and scenic. I had plunged over a cliff and was trying not to drown. The sharp contrast between my life and the lives of my friends—experiences which had previously felt so similar—was almost too much to take. Everywhere I looked, I saw what I should have had. I felt completely isolated and alone.

I was happy for each one of my friends. Of course I was. The last thing I would want was for one of them to suffer the way I was suffering. Of *course* I wanted their babies to live.

But I wanted my baby to live, too. And I thought that if the grief didn't kill me, the jealousy might.

Of the six of us, why did it have to be me? But also, why did it have to be any of us?

I was in survival mode, which for me meant a withdrawal from anything related to babies. I didn't want to see birth announcements. I didn't want to hear about "baby's first Christmas." Jealousy was tension in my shoulders and acid in my stomach. It was painful and embarrassing for me to want so desperately what others had.

Celebrity pregnancy announcements were a slap in the face. (Unless they were over forty or had struggled with infertility, in which case I could begrudgingly be happy for them.) *Teen Mom* and *I Didn't Know I Was Pregnant* made me blind with rage.

Pregnant women or new babies were my personal nightmare. And they were *everywhere*.

I saw a woman at Whole Foods carrying her infant in the exact same Graco car seat we'd selected for Eliza, the one with the black and white gingham that my mom had given to me at my baby shower a week before Eliza died. I got so lightheaded seeing it that I thought I might pass out next to the cheese display.

A local charity ran an advertisement featuring a little girl named Eliza, her name emblazoned across the bottom of the screen as she grinned and kicked a soccer ball. I watched that commercial as though I were searching for my own Eliza, then I wept for every piece of paper on which I would never get to write her name, for every item on which I would not inscribe her initials in permanent marker. To think there were parents in the world who cheerfully monogrammed the name "Eliza" on bibs and lunch boxes, who called out her name across playgrounds and backyards… I hated them because I was so jealous of their easy use of my baby's name.

My cousin had unexpectedly and unintentionally gotten pregnant a few months after I did. Her healthy daughter was born four months after Eliza died. I hoped that her baby would be healthy and alive, but several months later I saw a photo of my mother holding my cousin's baby, smiling down at a chubby little face on her lap. That image brought me to my knees, sobbing. We lost so much joy when we lost our daughter, so much happiness that we had hoped to share with our families. And everything we lost was something that someone else got to have.

I hated the way jealousy made me feel tense, every muscle in my body stiffening in an effort to protect my heart, my eyes growing hot with tears, my hands curling into fists. I had little capacity to be happy for other people, and it seemed to take a long time to revive that capability. Years later, I still feel a twinge of jealously toward anyone who gleefully announces a pregnancy without having previously experienced a loss.

Coping with new pregnancy announcements was especially difficult early in my grief. The summer after Eliza died, we were visiting David's grandparents for a family gathering. It had quickly become apparent that his family coped with difficulty by avoiding it, so I had prepared for this to be a struggle. We knew that they loved us, but his entire side of the family seemed incapable of coping with our grief, eager for us to move on. It had been five months since our baby died, and apparently that was long enough that they thought we should be functioning pretty close to normal (spoiler: I was not). They did not seem to consider that pregnancy might be a sensitive subject for us.

The reality was that once we were three months out from Eliza's birth, we had started trying (and failing) to get pregnant again, and I would have preferred to stick hot needles under my fingernails than be around pregnant women or babies. I also did not want to share this struggle with anyone—I didn't want anyone to know that we were trying to get pregnant again. We arrived at David's grandparents' house and had just carried in our bags and gathered in the kitchen when his grandmother announced another relative's second pregnancy with much delight: "And *this time* it was on purpose!"

I felt like the room was spinning. My vision got dark around the edges and the blood pounded in my head. I had to go lie down, and I called my mom from the basement guest room, stifling my sobs in a pillow. I claimed a migraine to get out of dinner, knowing I didn't have the energy to hide my grief and make conversation. I'd lost my appetite anyway. The next morning, his three-year-old niece accidentally called me "Mommy," and I walked into the bathroom, locked the door, and burst into tears, this time burying choking sobs in a hand towel.

Although they were a source of love and I know they never meant to be hurtful, just being together with our extended family was a struggle because all I could think about was the baby who was missing. I could so perfectly picture the person I would have been if our baby had been there with us, along with our niece and nephew. I would have been the mom with a five-month-old, showing off baby outfits and pushing a stroller on our walks. I would have been the aunt French-braiding my niece's hair while David's grandma held the baby, talking about what baby foods we would try first and asking David's grandmother and aunt questions about teething and nap schedules. I could easily imagine this happy, light-hearted, alternative version of myself. She was like a ghost at the periphery of my misery, but she also felt more real than this shattered, shaky grieving mother that I had become. I lost my baby and I didn't know how to be myself without her.

Jealousy wasn't about hating other people. I didn't wish them ill. I didn't want their babies to die. I just wanted a piece of what they had. I wanted their innocence. I wanted their self-assurance. I wanted my heart to feel light and easy again. I wanted pictures of my mom holding *my* baby. More than anything, I wanted my own baby in my arms. Instead, it seemed as though everyone else was getting what I wanted, and I was stuck on the outside looking in, my arms aching to hold my baby girl.

CHAPTER 15

It's not that I wanted bad things to happen to other people. It's just that I felt a little better when they did.

We don't have a word in English for what "schadenfreude" means. It's basically defined as pleasure derived from someone else's misfortunes.

It's uncomfortable to suggest that I got *pleasure* out of hearing about bad things happening to other people. I can't deny, though, that I found a sense of comfort in knowing that I wasn't completely alone in my suffering.

I would never *ever* wish someone else would suffer the loss of a child, but each time I would hear a happy birth announcement (and I heard *so many*, even while actively trying to avoid them!), it felt like one more fence separating me from the rest of the world. I wasn't sure I could ever go back, that I could ever celebrate new babies as I had before.

If you got bad news, though? I was your girl. And it was as though people seemed to know it. People began sharing things with me that they never had before.

Because I was so open about my loss and grief (it's pretty hard to keep an eight-and-a-half-month pregnant belly a secret, after all, and I had zero game face for a long time after), people seemed to understand that I was someone who would listen to their grief without judgment or some clichéd response. I found myself listening and connecting in unexpected moments with all kinds of grief experiences.

I mourned alongside our neighbor who woke up to find his husband dead next to him—a sudden heart attack in his forties.

I did my best to support a friend who was diagnosed with breast cancer in her 30s.

I talked about job losses, break-ups, infertility, and health concerns.

Divorces, diagnoses, family disputes, rejection, loneliness and fears of never meeting the right person... I found myself a confidante for people who were suffering. No matter how we were socially connected, we now seemed to be united, yoked in our grief. As fellow sufferers, we could abide each other's pain without trying to fix it, compare it, or dismiss its weight.

I have met bereaved parents who have argued that no one else can possibly understand what they are feeling—that no other grief equates to the loss of a child. I suppose there is truth in that claim. The grief I feel for Eliza's death is not quite the same as any other experience, no matter how devastating. Losing a child feels like the universe went back on its unspoken promise that children outlive their parents. But grief is also a universal human experience, and finding connection, even with those who had not lost a baby, became a means of navigating my own survival.

When people shared their grief with me—as long as they didn't compare it to the loss of a pet (which, yes, one person I know absolutely did this, making me realize I needed to shift that person to a more marginal role in my life)—it felt like they were trying to understand my experience. I saw them operating from a place of compassion, trying to relate my grief to their own, different experience.

(By the way: losing a beloved pet is sad and does cause grief. Dogs and cats are such special companions and their loss can be heartbreaking. We've had to say good-bye to Little Mac, and when I think of Cooper reaching the end of his days here with us, I'm terribly sad. It is nowhere near the same as losing a child, a partner, a parent, or a human friend. No comparison. Full stop.)

I noticed that many people tried to downplay or qualify their grief, not wanting to overstep. I had a friend tell me about an early miscarriage she'd experienced and then quickly add, "But I know it's not the same thing!" An early pregnancy loss is different from giving birth to a baby who died in the second or third trimester, but grief is not exactly a competition. There is no winner in this comparison contest. Any woman who has lost a pregnancy that she wanted understands the hopeful expectation, the pain of shattered dreams, the marking of time based on due dates that never came true. It's less about the same experience and more about how it feels to be lost, life having taken a sharp turn from the path we'd hoped to follow.

I also understood to some extent why someone would be afraid to connect our experiences—afraid of offending me, afraid of overstepping, afraid of letting themselves imagine how I might be feeling. Obviously no two grief experiences are identical, but I always appreciated it when people saw my sadness as a space for connection and not a freakish and unique experience that would forever mark me as separate and apart. When people shared pain they had experienced and talked about how they worked through it, it helped me feel like I was not an isolated freak. I hoped that others could understand and share my pain to some extent, and I appreciated that they were seeking a connection rather than trying to distance themselves from the horror of imagining a dead baby.

I think the bereaved parents I've known who resist that connection are those who need the enormity of their grief to be recognized as unique and therefore "unimaginable." Anything less would make them feel as though the magnitude of their loss was being diminished.

But I needed the magnitude to be diminished. It was filling up all the space in my life and it was suffocating me. I needed to see others who had lost loved ones—parents, spouses, dear friends—and who had found a way to go on. I needed their wisdom and compassion and company on the days I felt that I was drowning in my grief alone. And as I talked with others about different kinds of grief, I felt my own empathy expanding. I didn't necessarily know what it was to lose a spouse or a job or a parent, but I knew what it was to wake up with my heart pounding, to feel my limbs aching to hold someone else, to not even know who I was anymore. It wasn't so hard for me to connect with those who were suffering another kind of grief.

I think most people who have any imagination at all can imagine grief and find connection. They can't *know* our grief, and I don't expect them to. I wish nobody knew this grief of having your baby die. But I don't think that people should feel their grief experiences are incomparable. It's not a competition to measure whose grief is worse. It's a space for acknowledging disappointed hope and love with nowhere to go. I welcomed conversations that began with someone tentatively saying, "When my stepdad died, I had people tell me that I shouldn't be sad because he wasn't my 'real dad.'" Or, "My brother was 21 when he died. He was my best friend and I really spiraled out of control for a while." Or, "When my dad died, I had to cut back on my hours at work so I could cope." Or, "It took me three years after my mom died to feel like I was okay again." Or, "I had seven miscarriages before my son was born."

It's not exactly schadenfreude. Hearing these things didn't make me feel pleasure. The comfort didn't come from knowing other people are sad. The comfort comes from feeling less isolated. Pain and loss are great equalizers, and if we let them, they can bring us closer instead of dividing us.

Not everyone knows what it is like to lose a child (lucky bastards who remain blissfully ignorant). But most people know what it is to love someone who dies before they were ready to let them go. Many people have ached for someone to be part of a celebration they've missed. A lot of people have had their heart broken by someone they thought they could count on being there forever. Those people don't know exactly how I'm feeling, but they've got an idea. My grief… their grief… it's not so different. If there is one thing I've learned from all of this, it might be that we all walk around with big, gaping holes in our hearts.

As much as we don't want the people we love to die, we also know that if we didn't love them enough to grieve their loss, there wouldn't be a point to living at all. We can find connection through grief. What I began to realize, even in those early days when it seemed like I was plunging down through a bottomless pit of grief, was the other side of that truth: We're all connected by grief because we are all connected by love.

CHAPTER 16

A few months after Eliza's death, I was talking to a friend of mine about how hard it is to come to terms with the fact that everything I'd planned for my future was wiped out and now completely uncertain. I thought I knew what my life would look like, and now I had absolutely no idea.

She cautiously mentioned that she could relate on some level because her fiancé had called off their wedding. She had been several months into the wedding planning process—date and venue booked, wedding dress in the closet, flowers chosen, cake selected, invitations on order—when her fiancé quite suddenly broke up with her. She was not trying to compare her loss with mine—she added quickly that a break-up is not the same as the death of a child. But it was a relief that I could feel genuine sympathy for someone else. This was not a comparison game of who had it worse. It was relief to find a mutual understanding as we both grappled with sadness, loss, and uncertainty. I found some comfort in not being the only one who walked around fighting back tears, facing uncertainty and a persistent sense of shame. Being jilted by your fiancé is a private matter that feels like a public embarrassment, and it's all about losing the future you had planned on. The dreams and hopes you had, the idea of what your life was going to be like and who was going to be the most important person in it. All of that is suddenly gone in an instant.

And that is what losing a child feels like—it doesn't just hurt because someone you love is dead. It also hurts because it feels like a failure, like you must have done something wrong, something that others accomplish effortlessly. The death of a baby is also the beginning of what feels like an endless stretch of perpetual disappointment. It's not one event that you can move away from and get some distance on. The loss carries forward with you. All you planned, everything you had to look forward to celebrating (birthday parties and prom dresses and wedding receptions and family vacations and reading your favorite childhood books out loud) is suddenly blotted out. That part of your future is blank. Empty. And you're sitting there remembering so vividly what it felt like to be happy, and trying to reconcile the happiness that was so recent you can still taste it with the reality that it will never be yours at all.

I have come to think about this timeline as the double edge of grief. And I think anyone who has lost someone too soon must have felt it. Not only do you miss that person specifically—her personality, his laugh, the way he would have reacted to a particular situation, the advice she could have offered—you also miss the experiences you should have shared with him or her. The moments in your life that would have been brighter and sweeter if only you had shared them with your mom or your stepdad or your friend or your spouse or your big brother or your twin sister or your niece or your son or whoever it was who shouldn't have died so young.

Pregnancy is so often a time of planning, and while I was grappling with broken plans, the loss of hypothetical experiences, and an unimaginable future, I was also grieving the loss of this very specific baby girl and the person she would have become. I lost my newborn, but I also lost a mischievous toddler, a curious preschooler, and an elementary school kid with knobby knees and tangled hair. I lost a high school daughter making college visits and a young adult with whom I could navigate a friendship. When I miss Eliza, I miss the future we were supposed to have with her, but I also love her and miss her as a unique individual in a way I did not realize would be possible to feel for a baby who never breathed.

Sure, we projected onto her our own ideas of what she would be like when she was still our unnamed "Baby Duck," but there's also a way in which she was so intimately a part of David and me that I miss, and that no future children could ever replace. There were kicks and movements that felt like she was communicating with me—keeping me entertained during jury duty, distracting me while I was trying to lecture about Oedipus Rex, or connecting with me during our yoga classes. There will always be a place in my heart only she could fill. We will always wonder who she would have been, and we will always miss the tiny baby she was for such a brief window of time, and the girl she would have grown up to become.

Eliza's place in my world had seemed so secure. Now, everything was an unknown, and things that should have been familiar and comforting were reminders of how everything should have changed. What had we all talked about before I'd gotten pregnant? It seemed that every conversation I could remember had been about our baby, and about what we'd do with the baby this summer. Now there was no baby and I was hardly capable of conversation. She was gone, but I was also missing myself. I felt unrecognizable. I couldn't make sense of who I was without my daughter, or what my future would look like without her in it.

We miss our baby girl *and* we miss the people we would have been if she were here. No matter how good life gets—and at this point out, it is better than I ever could have imagined—there is still a part of me that appreciates all I have *and* misses the life we would have had if Eliza were here with us—even if I can't know what that would have looked like. This ongoing, perpetual loss is the double edge of grief, and we mourn not only our baby, but all the things our life might have held with her in it.

CHAPTER 17

When I was pregnant with Eliza, my best friend, Monica, was a newlywed and was enrolled in seminary. Monica was planning to come stay with me after Eliza was born in January, at the end of her long winter break, and help with the baby.

Instead, she came in December, right after her finals, at the start of her break, arriving a few days after Eliza died. She stayed with me in between visits from my parents. She picked up where my mom had left off—coaxing me to eat something, encouraging me to get off the couch and walk the dog. Even after she left, she called or texted me every single day for months. As you might suspect from someone who chooses to go to seminary, Monica was instinctively caring and compassionate. We had been friends for so long that we could do lots of reminiscing about life pre-pregnancy, so Monica brought the gift of conversations that didn't trigger tears. And she didn't have children, so that made it easier for me.

But Monica and her husband wanted children

and were, in fact, trying to have them. Obviously, as her friend, I wanted that for them as well. They were preparing for another round of IVF, having already had one failed and one canceled cycle, and I wanted to be supportive. I wanted Monica to get pregnant. I wanted her to be able to have a baby. There was no question about that.

It was complicated only because I *also* wanted to have a baby. Was there enough luck in the universe for both of us? Were we playing some zero-sum game I didn't know about? Yes, I wanted IVF to work for Monica. But also… where was *my* baby? Why couldn't this process be easy for Monica? Why did Eliza have to die?

Monica did get pregnant in her third round of IVF. It happened in April, three and a half months after Eliza died. It put her on a timeline remarkably similar to my pregnancy with Eliza. She was due at the end of December, where I'd been due in mid-January. I was so happy for her. And that happiness was accompanied by a rock of sadness in my stomach, jealousy twisting around my throat.

I wanted to be generous and encouraging. I wanted to be the same way I would have been if I weren't exhausted by the burden of carrying my own sorrow. I wanted to be supportive and sympathetic. I wanted to offer advice and talk about pregnancy and birth plans. But grief and bitterness were robbing me of my ability to be the friend I wanted to be—another kind of loss. And no matter how much I talked about it in therapy or how hard I tried, this bitterness was an obstacle I wasn't sure I could overcome.

My daughter died and I lost my ability to be fully and completely happy for my friend without my own grief and anger creeping in. I was grieving both of those losses.

At the time Monica told me about her pregnancy, David and I had gotten the okay from my doctor to start trying to have another baby. A few months later, it wasn't working. Not the first month we tried, and not the month after, or the month after that. I was getting increasingly desperate and increasingly jealous of everyone else in the entire world who was pregnant or parenting a newborn (which seemed to be virtually everyone).

It was hard for me to talk about pregnancy stuff, but I also felt awkward imagining that people didn't *want* to talk about pregnancy with me—like I was the Black Widow of Bereaved Motherhood. Like maybe my grief or my bad luck was contagious. Monica's daily texts or phone calls trailed off a bit later in the spring, which made sense as she was getting busy with the end of the semester approaching, but it felt like she needed to distance herself from me because I was her—and every pregnant woman's—worst nightmare. I was a walking reminder of what could happen to her. *Of course* she didn't want to talk to me daily. She wanted to talk about her pregnancy and wasn't sure how to do that with me. I felt defined by my grief. I had no other extracurricular activities. Sure, I was binge watching *Friday Night Lights*, which was a great filler for my evening hours, and Tami Taylor's hair gave me something else to feel mildly jealous about, but conversations about fictional football in Dillon, Texas could only go so far and I didn't have much else to say, especially if we were both trying hard not to talk about the thing we were constantly thinking about: pregnancy.

Monica had hosted my baby shower. She had driven in and, with the help of my local friends, had arranged for the perfect afternoon at a darling little tea shop, celebrating Baby Duckworth. We had a private back room and a super cute menu and they had all been so generous with their gifts. I felt so loved and so thrilled to be bringing a baby girl into the world who would grow up and have friendships like these. I'd laughed at the onesie Monica had given me that said "What the Duck?" with a rubber ducky on it. It had been an afternoon of big love and tiny sandwiches, a perfect baby shower with my friends.

I had hosted Monica's bridal shower at the country club in our hometown. I ordered invitations in her wedding colors and personalized napkins with her monogram. I worked with the other bridesmaids to make the menu plans. I ordered gorgeous flowers and her favorite desserts (no chocolate!) and we drank so much champagne that I had to call my parents to come pick me up from the afternoon shower, which of course we found hysterically funny.

This is what best friends do for each other, right? They celebrate each other. They throw the party and they add the details to make it special. They make the champagne toasts.

But now Monica was having a baby, and my baby was dead, and I wasn't pregnant, and I couldn't do it. I could not host her baby shower. I could not even attend. There was no way. Thinking about it made my throat tighten and my stomach lurch.

To be honest, part of me was angry that she would even *have* a baby shower. A party *after* the baby was born might have been fine, but how could anyone who knew me be confident enough to throw a party for a baby that wasn't yet born? It felt like a slap in the face. How could she possibly celebrate when she couldn't be sure her baby would be born alive? What made her think that *her* baby would live when my baby hadn't? Even as my rational brain understood that my loss should not keep anyone from celebrating her pregnancy, I felt angry that others seemed to feel entitled to a happy ending when it had been snatched away from me.

At the same time, I wanted to be there to celebrate this baby and Monica's hard-earned chance at pregnancy. I knew better than anyone that pregnancy outcomes could be unpredictable. What if this party was the only one her baby had? I was reminded by another babyloss friend that having a baby shower isn't necessarily saying that you're sure your baby will live. It isn't a show of entitlement or undue confidence. If anything, it's a gesture of hope and optimism. Forget the registry and the practicality of diaper gifts, it's a way of saying that you love this baby and you want to celebrate her life even before she is born.

I'd had two baby showers for Eliza, the one with friends in St. Louis and another in my hometown with family. They had each been sweet and special occasions, where I'd felt eager to bring my baby into this circle of love. After Eliza died, I felt almost like each event had been a cruel joke. I could hardly bear to think of the thoughtful gifts, the adorable decorations, the baby duck themes. To imagine watching someone else—even my best friend—sit with her round, pregnant belly, opening gifts and holding up tiny clothes for an unborn baby *who could still die unexpectedly*, everyone there smiling and blithely assuming that in a few short weeks she'd be using the diapers and swaddle blankets and onesie pajamas… my heart couldn't take it.

Fortunately, Monica's college roommate, Lindsey, stepped up where I fell flat. Lindsey hosted the party. I stayed home, the weight of guilt pressing me down into the sofa. I wasn't so much wishing I were there as wishing it weren't happening at all.

Lindsey hosted the party with enormous kindness and sensitivity. She sent me an invitation to the baby shower, but she enclosed it in a "thinking-of-you" card. She wrote that she understood the shower might be too difficult for me, but she wanted me to feel included. She wasn't sure if I would want to send a gift and there was no pressure to do so, but if I wanted to contribute, she'd be happy to purchase something and put my name on the card. She wrote that she was thinking of me and remembering Eliza. All of this was such a gift—that note, the care that she took when sending it to me, the thoughtfulness and understanding that came along with it. Perhaps most of all, seeing my daughter's name written out in the card. My bitterness might have crippled my ability to celebrate pregnancies, but it did not prevent me from appreciating kindness extended to me. I did send a check, asking Lindsey to add my name to whatever she purchased, and I remain grateful for the gracious way she acknowledged and made space for my grief.

CHAPTER 18

I had many friends show up for me in different ways, but I still felt lonely. I felt cut off and adrift, isolated by my sadness. I was desperate for connection, but a lot of the time I wanted to be alone. I didn't want to have to hide or minimize my suffering, but I hated how vulnerable it made me.

Most of the time when well-meaning friends would ask, "What can I do?" I didn't know what to say. (Now I know: Order pre-printed thank you cards. Go to the grocery store. Login to my email inbox and unsubscribe from every baby and pregnancy related email I was getting. Buy me some soft pajamas. Make some hot tea and sit with me in silence.)

One thing I knew I needed, though, was someone to let other people know what happened. I needed a friend to reach out to people who were somewhat in the periphery, but still important to my life. My financial advisor. The girl who cut my hair. The director of the writing program at my old job. The real estate agent we'd worked with. My dentist. People who were excited with me about this baby. People who would ask about her the next time they saw me. People whose faces would fall when I'd be forced to drop the "dead baby bomb" and tell them that she'd died. People who would feel awkward and uncomfortable when I couldn't stop crying after saying those words. I didn't want my daughter to be dead, but I also didn't want to have to tell people what happened, dropping this cloud of grief on them. It felt like an additional burden to bear. It reminded me of the sailor in Coleridge's creepy nineteenth-century poem *The Ancient Mariner*—not only did I have to experience "death in life," but I also had to walk around and tell my harrowing tale to every soul I met. This conversation was so painful and difficult for me that I wanted to avoid it at all costs.

I needed these people whom I saw regularly to know my baby had died, but I couldn't face telling them myself, so I asked my friends to notify people. My dentist forgot and cheerfully asked me about the baby a few months later (not at all awkward to mumble that my baby died around her gloved fingers in my mouth), but others responded immediately with empathy and concern, making disclosures that surprised and touched me.

I had a hair appointment that had been previously scheduled weeks before Eliza died. It was one of the few appointments standing on my postpartum calendar and I planned to have someone cancel it for me—what was the point of having cute hair when I was dead inside? But after my friend told her what happened, my hairdresser wrote me a handwritten letter telling me about her grief when her brother died and the difficulty she had coping with the loss of her only sibling and best friend. She closed by telling me that if I needed someone to talk to, she was "not afraid of grief."

I held that phrase close because it seemed to me to capture the way so many people responded to my tragedy. Glancing quickly away. Shifting awkwardly. Part of the reason I didn't want to go back out in the world was because I made people uncomfortable. People were afraid of me—or afraid of the depths of my grief, especially since I couldn't always keep it tucked away the way our society seemed to insist I should. Here was someone telling me that she wasn't scared of the very thing that most people I knew wanted desperately to avoid—my infinite sorrow.

I kept that hair appointment. As I looked at myself in her salon mirror that day, I was unrecognizable. My eyes were red-rimmed and hollow, my skin was pale, and my face looked like a stranger, but she treated me like she always had. The salon was nearly empty and the buzz of the hair dryers kept our conversation private as we talked about her brother and my baby. We both cried and hugged and became actual friends instead of friendly acquaintances that day.

I asked another friend to notify our financial advisor—a woman we met with once or twice a year to talk about retirement savings. I didn't expect to hear from her, but I didn't want to show up for a meeting in six months and burst into tears when she asked me how the baby was. She sent me a note, offering her sympathy but also sharing with me that her sister had a stillborn baby named Samuel, and describing the ways their family continues to remember him. This was a gesture that went beyond customer service. This was kindness, compassion, genuine humanity. And I held onto it with both hands, so desperate to cling to something good in a world that felt so dark.

At the time I lost Eliza, I was working part time, putting together adjunct teaching positions and tutoring jobs to save extra money for the months I planned to stay home with my baby. I tutored at a small learning facility directed by a brilliant and kind Japanese-American man in his seventies. We had become good friends in the few years that I'd worked for him, and he sent a short but sympathetic note to me after I emailed him to let him know we'd lost our baby and I didn't know when I would return to work.

My work at the learning center paid well and wasn't difficult, so it made sense for me to go back to doing that as well as teaching part-time at a university, but it was so, so hard for me to spend time with other people's small children after losing my child and what I feared at the time might be my only chance of having a baby. My growing belly and baby on the way had been the subject of countless conversations with parents at the center, and I dreaded going back and having to tell people who asked about the baby that she was dead.

Considering that it was nearly a year before I could talk about Eliza without crying, I also had no idea how I would manage to tell this story at work without making things supremely uncomfortable for many adults (including me), and potentially frightening for small children. I'm not sure whether the issue was generational, cultural, or just cluelessness, but my boss did not seem to think he needed to inform anyone what had happened—as though no one would ask about my baby and we could pretend it had never happened. Fortunately, the office manager and I worked together to draft an announcement to go out to all the families. Most of them apparently read it. The two parents who excitedly asked me how my baby was doing undoubtedly regretted *not* reading it.

One sweet woman whose children went to the center gave me a card with a note inside telling me that she had experienced the same thing and now she had two beautiful girls. I opened that card in my car after work and sobbed over that letter, so grateful that she had told me her story. I wanted desperately to see my future and to know whether I would ever be as lucky as she was. Most families were respectfully silent, which I honestly appreciated, as even the gentlest and most well-intentioned expression of sympathy overwhelmed me. I managed to nod and tried to smile when people offered condolences, and as soon as they had turned to go, I'd hurry to the restroom, trying to get into a stall before my tears spilled over.

Although I wanted people to know about Eliza, talking about her was incredibly hard for me. It was such a tender story to tell. I practiced a few times with my therapist one on one and with a grief support group, as we'd each go around and tell our baby's story as part of our introduction. Inevitably, though I could usually restrain the sobs, my throat would tighten and my voice would get unnaturally high, a giveaway for the tears that I was fighting desperately to restrain. I thought I was someone who could mostly keep a rein on my emotions, but when it came to talking about Eliza, I was at the mercy of my tears.

I practiced a short explanation: "We're not sure what happened, but our daughter was unexpectedly stillborn." But I couldn't say "stillborn" without sobbing. So I tried, "Unfortunately, we lost our daughter just before she was born."

It didn't matter how I said it. My sweet girl was dead. The baby I had dreamed of, hoped for, and planned my entire life around was gone. I could hardly talk about her, but also I didn't want to talk about anything else. I didn't even know who I was without her, and I guess that was the first thing I needed to learn: how to be myself if I wasn't Eliza's mom—at least, not in the way I wanted to be.

CHAPTER 19

As much as I missed Eliza, I also missed my old self. I wanted to be okay again. I knew that I would always grieve my first daughter, but I also wanted to find a way to move forward. The problem was at first that I didn't know how to feel hopeful after Eliza died. Perhaps I had confused hope with optimism, and I couldn't bring myself to be optimistic anymore. How could I expect that things would somehow be okay? I couldn't even imagine what okay would look like. Hope was something I used to know, something I wanted to find, but that existed just out of my reach. In retrospect, I think that once I moved past the bare minimum of survival, every morning that I got myself out of bed, showered and dressed, that was an act of hope. Life would move forward, regardless of whether I wanted it to. My hope was to find a way to make my life feel bearable.

The problem was that I couldn't fathom *how* life could get better. I couldn't bring Eliza back. Another child could never replace her. It seemed like I would be stuck forever. My grief felt like a life sentence from which I would never escape. One night I posted desperately to an online community of bereaved parents: "How long will it be until I stop crying every day?" One woman answered that it took her three or four months. Another said it was almost a year. I was grateful to get specific and concrete answers. It was far away, but there was an end to my tears in sight. Every day I cried was one less day I would cry. The pain wouldn't go away, these women told me, but it would shift. That was the best I could hope for.

It was fourteen months before I got through a day without crying. That means I cried at some point every single day for approximately 426 days. No wonder I was exhausted. Early on, hope was the thought that eventually I would get through a day without crying—a vague promise that things would eventually *feel* different even though my daughter would still be dead. I had to trust other mothers who assured me that would happen, even if I couldn't understand how.

The spring after Eliza died, we went to a Cardinals game with David's grandparents. His grandmother insisted on snapping a photo of us before we left for the game. I remember not wanting my picture taken. She later sent me a copy, and I threw it away. I look broken in that picture. I'm smiling, but the smile does not reach my eyes. My shoulders are slightly hunched forward, the position of someone recovering from a punch in the stomach, or bracing to receive one. David looks tired, his face shadowed by his ball cap, his smile strained. I don't think we wanted to go to the baseball game. It was something out of our old lives—a thing we used to do and kept on doing out of habit. So much of what I did in those early months felt empty, like I was going through the motions without feeling or experiencing anything.

I remember going to see a play—someone had sent us tickets. I love the theater, but as the date approached, I dreaded leaving my house. David insisted that we go, promising that I'd like it once we got there. We were unfamiliar with the show and had no idea that we would both end up hating it. It included a plot thread about a woman whose child had died and her entire family—including her other children—was wrecked because of it. It was probably the worst thing we could have sat and watched, and I can't for the life of me tell you why we didn't leave at intermission. It was like we didn't have the strength to make that decision. For some reason, we felt obligated to sit there, passive and miserable, because going to plays was something we used to like to do.

We kept forcing ourselves to do things that used to make us happy, even though they didn't feel like fun. And sometimes, they did offer us a bit of a reprieve. Sometimes pretending that things were normal was a kind of hopefulness. We were grasping desperately toward anything that might bring our lives back into color. And most of it didn't work. But still, we were moving forward, angrily, reluctantly, sadly… but forward.

I learned that hope for the future required me to reckon with the uncomfortable, heartbreaking reality that the future would look very different from the one I had imagined, and to somehow allow myself to trust that eventually I would be okay, even though I would still be grieving. I hoped my future would include other children, but I knew there were no guarantees.

Hope is what convinces you to try to get pregnant or to pursue adoption, but it is also what lets you set those dreams aside if you discover that parenting a living child in this life would require sacrificing too much of yourself—financially, emotionally, energetically—to continue along that path.

Hope is what takes you to that doctor appointment, as well as the baseball game or the theater. Hope is also what allows you to purchase a new novel, to sign up for a new exercise class, to dogear the page of a magazine, to make reservations at a new restaurant, long before you are convinced that you will ever enjoy those things. Hope may be a life-changing leap or a superficial decision, but even the smallest act is momentum that moves you forward. I felt myself grasping blindly for hope, unable to count on it, wanting something more certain. But this quiet, flickering idea that life would someday be better, even if I couldn't see what "better" would look like, was the thing that led us slowly out of the darkest places of our grief.

CHAPTER 20

I can't overstate how hard it was for me to feel a sense of hope again. My appetite for life was completely diminished. My energy levels were nonexistent. I didn't leave my house for weeks after Eliza died. I didn't want to go out, but also I had nowhere to go. I'd expected her to arrive in January, and my schedule was cleared for the December holidays and my maternity leave. My calendar, which should have been crowded with doctor appointments and infant CPR classes, and, later, nursing moms' groups and meet-the-baby visits, was completely blank. This was fine, because I couldn't imagine leaving my house. I didn't think I could handle ordinary interactions. How could I reply, "Fine," when someone asked how I was? How could I do anything but burst into tears, should the checker at the grocery store ask such a seemingly innocuous question?

Three weeks after Eliza died, we went to a grief therapy appointment. I knew therapy wouldn't cure my pain, but I had to do something proactive. I had to feel as though I were making progress and moving in some kind of forward direction, because otherwise I thought I might slip backward into a deep dark hole from which I'd never get out. I thought it might be more comfortable there, and that thought scared me.

I felt exposed and raw the afternoon we walked out of the house toward the car. My feet felt strange in shoes, my clothes still didn't fit. I had squeezed myself into normal clothes and put on makeup because I was desperate for the therapist to see some sign of who I had been before so she could help me get back there. The sidewalk was icy, and I clung to David's arm, but that had less to do with the weather and more to do with the fact that there was no way I could have propelled myself forward on my own. I felt like I could no longer function in the world of the non-bereaved. I was marked, set apart, and my grief made me feel so vulnerable and so brittle, like the smallest wrong thing would break me to pieces.

We sat side by side in the therapist's office, perching on a comfortable sofa as she sat facing us in a chair. She knew we were there because our daughter had died, but she asked us to tell her the whole story. David and I took turns talking. I found myself wanting to pour out all the details, wanting someone who didn't know us already to understand what we'd been through. I cried my way through several tissues, pulling them from the box on the table to the right, the fingers of my left hand threaded between David's fingers, clutching his hand like a lifeline.

She said all the right things, and she told me something I needed to hear. That she had worked with couples who had endured this kind of loss and that yes, they felt like life got easier. I couldn't see my way out of this misery, but I could trust this objective woman with a PhD when she promised me others had managed. I also felt like I could believe her when she said that one of the things that often makes life easier for couples whose child has died is having another one, giving our love another place to go. It helped me to hear this in a way that didn't sound like it was a betrayal to Eliza to want to continue to grow our family.

I'd gotten the name of this therapist from my OBGYN, and I went on to see her, first with David, and then on my own, for over a year. I needed someone to reassure me that I was making progress, and I needed someone to help me face my darkest fears and worst thoughts head on. I needed to know that I could feel as desperate and hopeless as I felt and still somehow trust that life would not always feel this bleak. I know there are many people who survive their grief without seeing a therapist—and I know that, unfortunately, without insurance coverage, the cost of therapy can be prohibitive. But whether counseling comes from a pastor, from the leader of a grief support group, or from a licensed therapist, I think that those of us who have benefited from therapy know that there is comfort in the wisdom of people who have worked with other grieving parents, and who also understand the psychology and spirituality of grief as a process.

As we drove to the therapist that first day, the snow we'd had earlier that month had partly melted into a grayish slush, but it was still bitterly cold outside. It was two days before Christmas and I was relieved that she could see us before the holiday. I knew that one session of therapy wasn't going to fix the ache in my chest, but I needed reassurance that we could survive this, and I thought it would help to hear it from someone with an advanced degree and years of counseling experience.

There were weeks when I would have notes in my phone about what I wanted to talk about with my therapist, and weeks when I would wonder if I should even go because I wasn't sure I'd have much to say. But each time I showed up, what I was doing was carving out time and space to face my grief head-on, to acknowledge my ongoing grief and the way its place in my life was continually shifting and changing—sometimes overwhelming, sometimes making space for other possibilities. Each time I sat on her couch, I had to work toward naming my experience, and wrestling what I was feeling into words somehow helped me cope with it. I got advice and feedback I could trust, and most of all the reassurance that I was doing the best I could and that what I was experiencing was normal for someone in my situation.

Finding the right fit with a therapist is important, and it can be an exhausting process. No one wants to sit down and bare their soul to a complete stranger only to realize an hour later that the weird vibe is still weird. But finding a therapist to help me understand my impulses and sort through my emotions, separating fact (Eliza's loss was literally the worst thing that had ever happened to me) from fiction (I would never, ever be able to recover from this) was crucial for me and my wellbeing.

CHAPTER 21

Eight weeks after losing Eliza, I went back to work. I did not feel ready, but I think if I'd waited until I was ready I might never have gone. I had intended to stay home for the spring semester with my baby, but after Eliza died, I notified people in my department at the university where I'd been teaching. A few weeks later, someone reached out to me and asked if I wanted to teach a freshman composition class three times a week starting in late January. I literally had nothing else to do. A reason to get myself out of bed, at least three times a week, seemed like a good idea. On the first day of class, though, I was reconsidering that decision.

The last time I'd been in a college classroom, I'd been a smug pregnant woman, handing back final essays and preparing to welcome my daughter to the world over winter break. Now I was returning empty-handed and broken-hearted. I was certain the students would sense my weakness. I was teaching two different classes on freshman writing, back to back, each one lasting an hour.

That first morning of class, I put on what would become my uniform: black stretchy pants and a baggy sweater. Then, with shaking hands, I put on a silver bracelet with Eliza's name spelled out on square beads. I was both terrified and hopeful that someone would ask me about it. (No one ever did.) I clasped a chain around my neck with a pendant that read, "Be brave, for I am with you always." I tucked it under my sweater. I did not feel brave.

I'd never met these students. They didn't know me. They didn't know that a few short months ago I'd experienced labor and delivery only to hold a dead baby. They had no idea that I was walking through life as a broken shell of myself. They only knew that they were assigned to my section of freshman composition. My stomach roiled with nausea, but I also felt compelled to get through the semester. I needed to know that I was still capable of doing this. It felt like something I had to do if I was ever going to move forward at all.

On campus on the first day of class, I went to the restroom near my classroom and hardly recognized my reflection. My eyes were red-rimmed, my mouth trembling. I was pale and my shoulders slumped. I still looked puffy from pregnancy, despite a complete loss of appetite since she'd died. As I looked at my pitiful face, I felt desperate to put on a show of confidence. I decided that I needed lipstick.

My coat pocket carried a red lip stain that I'd picked up at Target months ago—shortly before Eliza's death—and had never worn. I carefully outlined and then colored in my lips.

Smacking my lips together, I stepped back to get the full effect. Somehow, I had expected this to transform me into someone who looked confident and put together. Instead, I looked ridiculous. The lipstick was a bright, garish red that made me look even more pale. It *might* have been appropriate for a night out. It looked completely out of place on my drawn, sad face. Most of all, it was a bizarre choice for a class on a Monday afternoon with no other makeup.

I looked very cheap and rather silly. And I was about to go stand in front of a classroom of college students and try to get them to take me seriously.

Panicking, I grabbed some toilet paper and wiped my mouth. But this was a lip *stain*. The residue of this color was basically guaranteed to stay with me through my cup of coffee the next morning. All I managed to do was smear the outline slightly, giving me the look of someone having an allergic reaction, as though hives were beginning to break out around the mouth and lips. It was almost laughable, except that I was miserable.

And now I had to go to class, my lips a garish red, my cheeks pink with embarrassment.

I looked stupid. But I still got through class. And I was distracted for a moment from my sadness. I was now a human person feeling silly—not just a bereaved mother feeling devastated. I stood in front of the class, raw and vulnerable, and I went through introductions and the syllabus as I had always done. I remembered how to do this. I could do this and be sad at the same time. I could even compartmentalize my sadness a little bit, pushing it off to one side of my brain so that I could focus on the task at hand. It was like exercising a different muscle, a different part of myself. I was more than my grief and I could access this other part of myself while I was teaching.

I still felt more vulnerable than I ever had in a classroom. Each day on my drive in, I had to take deep breaths to prepare myself. The hot weight of tears was always right behind my eyes. But in a way, my grief also made me focused and bulletproof. I had a new perspective about class. I wanted to teach what mattered. I had no tolerance for rude or disrespectful behavior—toward me or anyone else in the class. Life was fragile and fleeting and I was not going to take crap from anyone. At the same time, we were all going to treat each other gently.

I kept my loss a secret from them. I pretended for an hour in front of each class that I was a reasonably competent instructor and not someone whose life had imploded. Each class period was difficult, but it was also a relief. It was a space to act and be outside of and separate from my loss. It was a space in which I wasn't defined by my grief. It also took a great deal of energy for me to act "normal" for two hours. Each day, I got through class, then hurried out to my car. I'd duck into the driver's seat, ensconced in the shadows of the parking garage, and burst into tears, leaning on the steering wheel to sob before driving home. I had to cry because I missed her so very much, because I was barely holding it together. I basically collapsed into my car, exhausted from putting on the façade of a non-grieving, fully functional person.

While teaching felt like an act—pretend to be normal, put on my professorial persona, fake it to make it through the class—it was also an important reminder of something inside me that was more than or other than a bereaved mother. Much of the time, my grief felt as though it had completely subsumed my personality, but in the classroom, I could access this other part of my mind and do something productive three times a week. This distraction turned out to be surprisingly helpful.

Because my students didn't know that I was a bereaved mother, there were no expectations about how well I was or was not coping, so I never felt like I was being judged by them—except maybe whether I was a boring instructor. As tiring as it was, I liked getting absorbed in the moment and caught up in lecturing or leading discussion. When I was focused on teaching, my brain had a break from the constant loop of grief, the replay of those traumatic hours in the hospital, or the ongoing rehearsal of "what should have been." In front of the classroom, in order to do my job, I had to think about something besides my baby and my broken heart and ruined life.

There were days when I resisted all of it, dreading my teaching time and crying on the way to school. There were also days when I cut class a few minutes short because I could feel myself reaching a breaking point. But there were more moments when my students delighted me with their insights or observations about a reading assignment. There were times when they laughed at my nerdy jokes, or I felt genuine interest in their research, and I felt human again. There were days when I felt like a good teacher, and I needed so desperately to feel good at *something* since my entire experience with motherhood still felt like an enormous failure.

Although I never talked about Eliza with my students, that semester was healing for me in other ways. I wasn't putting on a show of pretending I knew what I was talking about. I shared what I knew and admitted what I didn't. We talked about writing, image, and the impossibility of perfection. One day, a student was being disrespectful and I asked him to leave the class—something I would have never had the nerve to do before. My hands were shaky and my heart was racing, but my voice was level as I asked him to take his things and go. He wrote me an apologetic email explaining that he hadn't meant to be disrespectful to me. Perhaps it was an overreaction on my part, perhaps it was a lapse of judgment on his part, but I asserted myself, knowing that life was already too hard to have to put up with nonsense from students.

I don't know if they sensed how thin was the veneer of capability that masked the total wreck of a person I was inside, but somehow we made it through the semester. I was pleasantly surprised by the excellent teaching evaluations I got from the students at the end of the term. I was the weakest and most broken version of myself, but I was also genuinely glad to be back, and I think the students sensed that. Without knowing it, those students saw me through the worst months of my life and they helped me start to find my way back to myself.

They also saw me wear red lipstick only once, and we never spoke of it again.

CHAPTER 22

Being back at work gave me a sense of control and mostly made me feel like I was capable and competent. But unexpected conversations took their toll, and I only felt in control if I felt like I was successfully hiding my grief. Anytime I needed to talk about Eliza, I was undone, but fortunately I was able to control most of the conversations I had at work. My colleagues knew what had happened and were polite and respectful. My students were mostly new, so they had no idea I'd been pregnant a year ago. When I wasn't teaching, I mostly kept to my office. Social pleasantries were still difficult, and it was easier to avoid people.

One day in early fall, I decided to take advantage of the free lunch for faculty and I went to the dining hall. I was standing at the salad bar and realized that I was behind a student who had been in my class the semester I was pregnant with Eliza. He was a basketball player, a decent writer. He had curly brown hair. I hadn't seen him since that semester. He made a spinach salad and then handed over the tongs so I could scoop up my spinach leaves.

As he did so, he said, "Oh, hey Dr. Taylor. How's the baby?"

And right there at the salad bar, with a pane of glass separating me from neatly sliced vegetables and brightly colored shredded cheese, with the chatter of students all around me, with fluorescent lights overhead and a college kid in basketball shorts standing next to me, I had to say out loud in carefully measured ones, "Oh. Well, we had very sad news. We lost the baby."

I said it while focusing on pinching green spinach leaves between plastic tongs and transferring them to the white bowl on my tray. I did not look up at his face. I concentrated on keeping my breath steady. I willed myself not to cry.

He said that he was so sorry, his voice low and sad.

Feeling uncomfortable with his obvious discomfort, I tried to keep my voice light. "Yes. It's been really rough." Then, I forced myself to add, "Thank you for asking, though. I'm just glad the semester has started and I can try to get back to normal."

I was lying to him so that he wouldn't feel terrible for asking me a polite question and getting a dead baby bomb in return.

The idea of getting back to normal was so ridiculous, so impossible. I wanted to throw my tray and that salad to the floor and run sobbing out of the dining hall. Instead, I forced a tight smile in his direction. I walked by the tables full of other faculty, nodded a brief greeting, and sat down at a small table by myself. My throat was tight and my eyes felt hot. I gulped water, trying to compose myself. I grabbed a novel from my bag—my best means of defense against unwanted conversation and escape from undesirable reality.

It was too late. One conversation had been too much. My hands were shaking. My eyes were full of tears threatening to spill over. My appetite was gone.

I ate two bites of salad before giving up. I put my tray on the conveyor belt, gathered my things, and headed back to my office. I closed the door behind me, locked it. Kept the lights turned off. Sat at my desk, staring at the sunshine filtering in between the dusty miniblinds. I cried silently, tears streaming down my cheeks.

Why did this have to be my story? Why did I have to be one whose baby had died? Why did this have to happen to me?

I had fifteen minutes before I needed to teach English composition to first year college students. I already knew from experience that it was enough time to fall apart and put myself back together.

CHAPTER 23

The semester before Eliza died, I taught Mary Shelley's *Frankenstein* to college students in a literature class. As I tell my students, Mary Shelley is fascinating to begin with—she wrote her most famous novel when she was still a teenager, hanging out with famous romantic poets (and having an affair with the man who would become her husband). Her mother (Mary Wollstonecraft Shelley) was an eighteenth-century feminist who wrote "A Vindication of the Rights of Women" in 1792 and died from complications of childbirth a few years later, after giving birth to her only daughter. Mary Shelley herself had four children and only one of them lived to grow up.

In 1816, Mary Shelley got married, had a stillborn daughter, and wrote the first draft of *Frankenstein*. She was nineteen years old.

When I taught the novel, I spent a lot of time pointing out the book's obsession with the link between the marriage bed and the death bed. Repeatedly, the novel presents this troubling connection. Dying parents beg their children to get married, murders take place on wedding nights and wedding sheets become shrouds, dreams problematically confuse mothers, monsters, and wives. I discussed these themes as I stood in front of my class, my belly full of squirming baby, and gave my students a brief biographical and historical outline of Mary Shelley's life. I pointed out that the novel was written by a woman whose mother died after giving birth to her, and who had recently experienced the death of her own baby, a stillborn little girl. Death and birth were undoubtedly bound up together in her experience.

I vividly remember standing by the dry erase board, sunshine streaming in the second-floor classroom windows, saying something like, "This overlap between birth and death and marriage beds in *Frankenstein* is perhaps less surprising in the context of the nineteenth century, when the rate of women and children dying in childbirth was much higher than it is today."

I paused and then patted my round, pregnant belly and said with a broad smile, "Thank goodness, right?" My students and I laughed together.

Babies—and their mothers—died in the nineteenth century for lots of medical reasons. We couldn't peek inside the womb and see placenta previa or growth restrictions. We didn't have prenatal vitamins or Doppler machines. C-sections were dangerous. In-utero diagnoses were impossible. Childbirth was a gamble of life and death wrapped up in an experience that promised joy, guaranteed pain, and always came with a well-known risk.

That was two hundred years ago. When doctors inadvertently caused infections that killed people because *they didn't know to wash their hands*. Today? In this age of modern medicine? Babies and mothers don't die. I said as much to my students. I was that sure of myself.

I know now that some of my self-assurance came from my unearned privilege as a white mother with access to quality health care, whose concerns would be taken seriously by my doctors. But I could not predict the outcome or protect my baby. Of course, I was aware there were some inherent risks. I just thought they were small. I thought that I could do enough to keep my baby safe.

In teaching *Frankenstein*, we talked a lot about monsters, about the piecing together of body parts, and about who the real monster is in the novel (spoiler: it's the scientist, not his creature). I remember preparing for class and making note of the definition of the word "chimera," which comes up often in the analysis of monsters in literature.

> **chi·me·ra** (kī'mirə,kə'mirə/) *noun* 1.(in Greek mythology) a fire-breathing female monster with a lion's head, a goat's body, and a serpent's tail. 2. a thing that is hoped or wished for but in fact is illusory or impossible to achieve. 3. an individual, organ, or part consisting of tissues of diverse genetic constitution

One word with multiple and diverse definitions. A chimera can be a monstrous woman, an impossible dream, or a genetic combination of separate parts (like Frankenstein's monster). We talked about Victor Frankenstein's ambition, how he creates a chimera both in the pieced-together creature and in the illusory dream of power and immortality.

Months later, I was surprised to discover that this word also comes up in scientific discussions of pregnancy, in relation to fetal cells that remain in mothers' bodies. Scientists suggest that the fetal cells from the baby may function as a means of protection or renewal for the mother's organs. Laura Sanders writes in *ScienceNews*, "Her cells slipped into your body and your cells circle back into her. This process, called fetal-maternal microchimerism, turns both mother and child into chimeras harboring little pieces of each other."

I was grieving my daughter when I read the *ScienceNews* article. I was not thinking about Frankenstein's uncomfortable juxtaposition of birth and death. But when I read about the cellular symbiosis of pregnancy, I did a double take at the word "chimeras." I found it strangely comforting that Eliza was still a physical part of me, that she and I were joined together at the cellular level.

And my mind went back to the other dictionary definition: "a thing that is hoped or wished for but in fact is illusory or impossible to achieve."

She was my chimera, my impossible dream. I'd had every reason to believe it would come true, only to be bitterly disappointed. And now, I'm here without her. Her cells are still swirling around with mine, but I can't hold her or squeeze her or breathe in her soft baby smell. I want to wrap her up in my arms, but at the same time, I haven't let go of her at all. I couldn't. Because she has knit her way into my physical reality, and nothing could extricate her cells from mine—not even death.

CHAPTER 24

I was a week or two into my grief sentence, a week or two out from Eliza's death. I was curled up on the couch in the living room. I spent so many hours of those days curled up, my spine a shell trying to protect my broken heart. The television was on and I was gazing blankly in that direction, so I suppose I was watching TV. It was a rerun of *Saturday Night Live*. It was an old skit—the one with Alec Baldwin talking about schweddy balls—and suddenly, it made me laugh.

I was mere days out from the death of my firstborn daughter, and laughter somehow escaped from my mouth. The sound was nearly unrecognizable to me, bubbling up from a place I thought no longer existed. It was a fraction of a second, but it was there. I'd been briefly, temporarily distracted from my sorrow. By Alec Baldwin's schweddy balls.

I wasn't sure how it was possible for me to be gutted by grief and still giggle at *Saturday Night Live*. I had never experienced that kind of paradox before. I felt guilty that something so stupid—schweddy balls—had offered me a glimpse of something beyond grief. But that fleeting moment had been such a relief.

Even now, it feels disloyal to say that I felt happiness after Eliza died. Maybe happiness wasn't the word for it. The best I could hope for were little pockets of time when I felt almost like my old self. At first, the most I could hope for was the fog of grief lifting enough that I didn't feel physically ill. But then, something would spark a flicker of interest, and I would feel like maybe I could reclaim my life—like grief would be a part of it without being the whole of it. I remember paging through a magazine several weeks after Eliza's death. A friend had dropped off a fashion magazine, along with some flowers and a chocolate bar. I had no interest in a fashion magazine, but it was something to do, so I was going through the motions, absently flipping through the pages. Then, as though I might want to return to it again, I folded down the corner of a page that featured a beauty editor's recommendation for eyeshadow.

When I realized what I'd done, my breath snagged on my teeth. My daughter was dead, and I thought I might be interested in trying this eyeshadow? Somehow, both things were true.

It was an uncomfortable paradox.

It seemed like I hadn't even been *thinking* about Eliza when I dog-eared the magazine page. Had a few seconds of my life gone by without me thinking about her? Had I *really* gotten distracted by an article about new cosmetics for spring?

And was this hopeful? Or heartbreaking?

There was a part of me that felt guilty about feeling a superficial interest in something like eyeshadow. It was so silly and pointless in the greater scheme of things. But, oh, I missed silly and pointless. I was *so tired* of deep and heavy. I spent so much of my time aching for my baby and thinking about love and life and afterlife and souls and cells and faith and doubt. My brain was exhausted by the philosophical exercise that ran incessantly. And now, here I was, thinking about eyeshadow instead of the inscrutable mysteries of the universe. I felt guilty. And I felt relieved.

Nothing would bring back Eliza. No punishment I inflicted on myself would return my daughter to me. No consideration of philosophy or metaphysics or faith and religion would bring me full and complete comfort when all I wanted was her in my arms now. And whatever the promises of "retail therapy," materialistic indulgence would not lighten my grief. But if I could find a space to experience a momentary happiness on a superficial plane of existence... was that wrong?

I hoped not. Because it suddenly seemed like it might be possible for eyeshadow to offer me a tiny distraction, and I thought maybe I should take happiness where I could get it, even if it was fleeting and superficial. It occurred to me that this might be the only kind of happiness there was left for me. My deepest, most primitive desire—to be Eliza's mom, to actively parent her and raise her and see the person she would become—was lost forever. I didn't know if peaceful contentment would ever be possible with her gone from me. The best I could do at this point was to try to make this heart-wrenching existence without her as tolerable as it could be.

I started to make space for tiny pockets of happiness. Small things I could look forward to each week. Nothing that made me feel completely happy, joyful, or content, but small distractions that could fill the void of nothing to look forward to, no future I could look to with certainty.

There was a lot of Netflix. I spent some time thinking about foods that might tempt my appetite back into existence and found a new place for Chinese takeout. New books. Soft, stretchy pants. We even took a trip to Florida over spring break. It wasn't *fun*—nothing takes the fun out of lounging by the pool with a drink quite like the broken-hearted wish that you were at home with a three-month-old—but it had its moments of happiness. A spring training baseball game in the sunshine with a cool breeze. A sunset walk on the beach, writing her name in the sand. An elegant dinner overlooking the ocean, with talk about our tentative hopes for our future and maybe even having another baby.

Nothing in this world could make up for losing Eliza, but I knew that I needed to work toward appreciating the beauty that the world still had left. Otherwise I'd be living this black and white and gray version of life forever. Otherwise I'd miss out on everything. I wanted Eliza to feel my love, but I didn't want her to have caused me permanent misery.

Jack Gilbert writes, "We must have the stubbornness to accept our gladness in the ruthless furnace of this world." I took that quote to heart, thinking often about how painful and tragic this life could be, and how we must hold on to whatever slivers of happiness we can find. And this is what I tried to do. It took effort—immense effort at times. Gratitude is a practice and after my daughter died, it was one I had to force. I would frequently second guess myself. I would circle back to misery. I would have a happy day and spend the next day crying until my eyes swelled nearly shut. I would be feeling good and then I'd read another babyloss mama's blog post and my grief would rush up and overwhelm me. I would unleash my feelings of guilt and uncertainty upon my therapist, needing to be reassured that making plans to have lunch with a friend and *looking forward* to that lunch did not mean that I was leaving my daughter behind. I would hold out hope that I'd get pregnant again, and fear that this would mean Eliza would be forgotten.

I did not need my daughter to die in order to understand suffering or to experience gratitude. But Eliza's life forced that practice of happiness to the forefront of my mind every single day. I was grieving the greatest loss I'd ever experienced, and I was taking deep breaths of gratitude for an understanding spouse, a handwritten note in the mail, a tree that didn't bloom but finally leafed out in green, a lazy dog at the end of a leash on a warm spring evening, a dinner out on our deck, another Maisie Dobbs novel.

These pockets of happiness weren't waiting for me. I had to make them happen. I had to be stubborn enough to find those moments of gladness in the ruthless furnace of my life after loss. I had to build something up from the ashes so that I could stand to go on without her. The weight of my grief was unbearably heavy, and so I had to learn how to balance it. I had to let laughter back into my life without it feeling like a betrayal. I had to hold happiness and grief in the same hand, understanding that it wasn't about choosing one, but finding a way for them to coexist forever.

CHAPTER 25

At first, it took a great deal of effort and energy to redirect my thoughts and think about anything besides my grief. The last thing I wanted to do was relive those gut-wrenching moments of anguish in the hospital room, but my mind would replay those hours as though searching for a place to go back and do something that would change the outcome. Although I had been overwhelmed with exhaustion at first, as the weeks went on, I came to dread going to bed. I would stay up late watching mindless television, my tired eyes burning, because I needed to fall asleep without pausing and falling into my own thoughts. I had the TV on almost constantly—something that previously I would have found irritating. I needed the distraction of someone else's dialogue to drown out what was going on in my own head.

Eventually, and with the encouragement of my therapist, I landed on another distraction: redecorating my house. In the previous months and years, I hadn't paid much attention to furniture or décor. We were living on

David's teaching salary and my graduate school stipend, so there wasn't a lot of extra money. We made do with inexpensive, second hand furniture, cobbled together hand-me-downs. I had been focused on finishing my dissertation and preparing for the baby, so except for decorating her nursery, I hadn't put a lot of thought into what I wanted our house to look like. David had come with plaid couches, so plaid couches were what we had.

Working part-time with no social life and no baby to care for left me a lot of time at home. And when thinking about would-have, could-have, should-haves became too unbearable, I would start thinking about the house. Someone gifted me a subscription to *US Weekly* and to *Better Homes and Gardens*, and both proved to be excellent distractions. When I'd close my eyes and see the hospital room, I'd refocus my brain by looking at Pinterest living rooms, or Craigslist furniture, or envisioning how I could repaint or re-purpose something we already had.

I didn't feel fully invested in any of it—part of me would circle back to the idea that "none of this matters anyway" because nothing mattered since my baby was dead—but I also welcomed the opportunity to put my brain to work on something besides second guessing exactly when the last moment was that I felt Eliza move and what might have happened if I'd realized that her movements had changed. I could easily torture myself with such questions. Now when they started churning, I redirected toward curtain panels and coordinating paint swatches.

I slipcovered our sofa—the plaid one that we'd moved from my husband's bachelor apartment to the house we bought together, the one I was sitting on when I realized that my cramps were more than Braxton Hicks and I needed to go to the hospital. Erasing the plaid didn't erase the pain, but at least that pattern wasn't there to give me flashbacks. Then I started saving for a new sofa and eventually I sold the old set on Craigslist, relieved to have that reminder (and the plaid upholstery) out of my house.

Although I was fiercely protective and sentimental about many of Eliza's things, I was more than happy to get rid of things that reminded me of the "before." Rearranging my living room was pointless, yes, but it made me feel better when the room looked and felt different than it had when I'd initially imagined putting a bassinet next to the couch. I needed the room to look different. It was mostly a superficial and materialistic practice, but it was also somewhere to put thought and energy. It offered immediate gratification and something else to keep my mind busy.

I'm certainly not alone in seeking projects and distractions in the wake of loss. Some of the other bereaved mothers I met became runners or returned to running in the wake of their grief. Although I'm not a runner, I can understand that urge to push your body, to clear your head, and I'm sure the endorphins are an enormous benefit. Some women turn to art, and create gorgeous paintings or hand-lettered signs, often honoring their babies. I ordered a photo of Eliza's name written on the beach at sunset, created by a bereaved mother who is also a talented artist and photographer. Another friend of mine discovered she has an incredible talent for cookie baking and decorating, spending hours tracing and filling sugar cookies with elaborate frosting designs. I preferred to paint walls and refinish furniture, letting the mindless brush strokes soothe me even if I often dissolved into tears, thinking that I never could have completed this project if I had a baby crawling around, into everything.

Whatever the project, whatever the distraction, I craved a way to fill the hours and the days with something besides my heartache. It wasn't a way to feel *better*—although I was desperate for that. It was a way to feel something different, or to get in the zone and feel nothing at all for as long as possible. Grief doesn't come with an off switch, but I found that occasionally, I could hit the pause button for a few minutes at a time.

CHAPTER 26

The greatest balm for my grief was not a distraction, but a membership. I was a member of the club that no one wanted to join, and I needed to find my people. The only thing that could convince me that my grief was endurable was to know others who had and were enduring it.

I needed someone to tell me, *You are not alone.* That is perhaps the only sentence in the English language that offered me any kind of real comfort after Eliza died.

I received many sweet notes and cards in those early, awful days of grief. The ones that meant the most to me, that buoyed me up when I was sinking to my lowest under the breathtaking weight of grief, were the ones in which the writer would share their own story of loss and how they survived it. One of these was from Norlene, the mom of my childhood best friend Erin. Norlene wrote to me about her son Adam, Erin's younger brother, who had died shortly after he was born. Erin and I had talked about Adam in the hushed tones of children who know they are talking about something important without fully understanding the weight of it. I did not know any details about how he had died, and I had never heard Erin's parents talk about him. Norlene wrote to me, in her remarkably beautiful penmanship:

To go home from the hospital without the baby that you've poured all your thoughts, hopes, dreams and love into—is probably the hardest thing you will ever have to face.

But with that devastation comes unlimited love. The bond between a husband and wife who go through the loss of a child can be even stronger than it was before. This is a time that only the two of you can truly share together. The raw pain and utter emptiness for each of you will recede with the deep love of the other. This is a tragic event in both of your lives and only the two of you will ever know the depth of the feelings involved. That piece of your personal histories will pull you closer together forever.

I needed this. I had heard the troubling statistics about how many marriages don't survive the loss of a child, but this was the first time I had been told that our grief could also solidify our love. I held those words as a promise, a guarantee that my marriage could remain intact. Even in the sticky black sadness of those first few weeks, I felt my connection with David deepen, and I was grateful to see the possibility of our love lasting echoed and affirmed in her letter, as well as demonstrated in her 30-plus-years of marriage.

I heard from my older cousin Angela, who had also had a stillborn daughter, Brittney. Brittney was born fourteen years before Eliza. I had been a teenager at the time, and Brittney's death did not register with me the way it should have. I felt sad for Angie, of course, but at sixteen years old, I did not consider the depth of her grief, nor the lasting impact of Brittney on Angie's life. Angie emailed me and I read her words again and again, grateful to know someone who had walked this path and found a way to carry her grief gracefully. Not unlike my preteen years when I admired Angie for having a fantastic perm and the most fashionable clothes, I now looked to her as a role model showing me that I could be something other than the crumbled and emotionally crippled person I was in that moment. Angie wrote:

> *For me...I remember feeling like I was the only one who ever knew her and I was so sad over that fact. I remember sleeping with her little stuffed animals around me and her baby blanket stuffed down my shirt right next to my heart for days. I would take the little clip of her hair and just stroke it. I looked at her pictures and would sob so uncontrollably I couldn't breathe. I would go from feeling strong to feeling devastated, feeling at peace to getting so pissed off I called my pastor and told him God sucked-ass! (I still can't believe I cussed at a minister). I overturned tables, chairs,*

broke things and then found a sense of relief in picking everything back up and re-organizing. I thought I was going crazy with the roller coaster of emotions I rode. I blamed myself thinking I had to have done something wrong and had the hardest time coming to terms with the fact that I couldn't have done anything different and had a different outcome. I just needed desperately for things to make sense! But I think that just as the reason this happened doesn't and can't make sense, the way we deal with it doesn't make sense. Healing and acceptance is a process and it's ok to do it in your own way.

And eventually it doesn't ache like it does now, and in time you will be ready to do it again, as scary as that may seem now.

I needed to hear that reassurance from someone who had been there—that we could try again and have another baby, despite our fears.

I received a card from my great aunt Sue, whose first baby girl, Jerry Sue, died shortly after she was born. My aunt Sue wrote in her card that she was so sorry and that I should "turn to God." I didn't know exactly what that meant or how to do that, but I figured she was probably repeating the same advice that she'd gotten. I was struck with sadness, though, because I had never heard about Aunt Sue's little Jerry Sue, a baby girl who would have been the same age as my father. I wondered now how hard it had been on Aunt Sue when her sister had a baby, my dad, a few weeks after Aunt Sue buried her daughter. I wondered whether it had been possible for her to watch my dad grow up and not measure his milestones against everything her baby girl never got to do. I wondered if she felt like her baby was something she couldn't talk about.

As I became aware of people in my life who had lost a pregnancy or survived the death of a child, I also started googling and making lists of famous people who had lost a baby. I needed physical evidence that people survived this. Jacqueline Kennedy. Katey Sagal. Mary Shelley. Lily Allen. Josephine Baker. Linda Evangelista. And more. I needed this promise that it could be me, too. I needed to know that her grief could shape me without being the only thing that defined me.

In the weeks that followed Eliza's death, I wrote about her, our loss, and my grief on my blog. Although my blog posts were raw and honest, I didn't have many qualms about posting my experience publicly. Somehow it felt easier to confess to strangers than to real people. Wrestling with language to try to find the right words to express how I was feeling also made me feel like I could contain the grief, a little bit, at least in the time it took to write something. Struggling to put grief into words offered me a marginal sense of control in this otherwise spinning world. I couldn't fix this, I couldn't undo, but I could *name* it. I could try to express what otherwise threatened to pull me under. And before long, I started getting comments from other bereaved parents.

I would follow links from the comments and read other blogs, leave my own comments. I started to connect with some other moms and a couple of dads. Some were on a similar timeline of grief, having lost a child within months of Eliza's death; others were a little bit ahead of me and could offer a glimpse of a life in which maybe I wouldn't feel like I was perpetually suffocating from sadness. Some of us began to email frequently, our messages functioning like a lifeline.

Finding my tribe of babyloss parents was a healing connection like no other. I was now part of a cohort set apart for the worst and most shocking of reasons, and yet I also found myself a member of a group of women that were also vibrant, brilliant, funny, silly, and selfless, and who were also physically sick from grief, fearful that they caused their baby's death, unsure how they would move forward in this world that no longer had their child in it. Recognizing these traits in other bereaved mothers made me consider that perhaps my entire self hadn't died alongside Eliza, even if my old self was overshadowed by my grief.

Perhaps there was a way to get back to some resemblance of the person I had been before. Naturally, I would be changed forever, but maybe that change didn't have to be a brutal erasure of all the things that had once been fun and easygoing. Maybe I could believe these people who promised me that I could find a way out of my grief and still take my love for Eliza with me. Maybe her death didn't have to be the end of my life, but could in fact be woven into it, could become a vital part of my story without being the *entire* story.

This connection with my tribe didn't happen overnight. It developed slowly and organically over several months and, in some cases, even years. I emailed so often in the early months that I literally rubbed the lettering off my laptop keyboard from typing so fast and frequently, but those emails were lifelines. We wrote about our babies, we wrote about our grief, our regrets, our guilt and shame. We wrote about our husbands, our hobbies, our families, our heartache. We wrote about vacations that were misery transplanted in another place, and vacations that made our hearts feel a little lighter. We shared secrets and made confessions and did our best to comfort one another. We sent cards and flowers to commemorate each other's babies. We encouraged each other in times of stress and change—moving, going back to work, adopting a puppy. We made each other laugh. As subsequent pregnancies or adoptions occurred, we supported and counseled each other as best we could. We discussed the superficial (the stretchiest yoga pants so that you didn't have to wear maternity wear after your baby died) and the serious (how to deal with thoughtless coworkers upon returning to work).

My friend Sarah and I connected through my blog and then began exchanging email after email. It gave me a measure of hope to imagine that wherever my Eliza was, she was with Sarah's baby Otis. That somehow, they were together on the other side of the stars, that they had connected just as their mamas had. In this way, Eliza's community expanded along with mine... Otis. Andrew. Jack. Hayes. Cale. Anna. Addison. Max. Olivia. Julius.

Love. Caroline. Hope. Camille. Aiden. Bear. Elizabeth. Alexander. Liam. Evelynn. Alana.

As time went on, I met—online and in real life—more and more parents who were grieving, and I added their babies name to the list of those with Eliza: Andy. Avalon. William & Ethan. Ava. June. Katie. Baby Boy Springer. Logan. Thaddeus. Aliya & Bennett. Scotlyn & Reese. Jonah. Matthew. Josephine. Madelyn. Larkin. Lydia. Annalise & Emmalyn. Luke. Kathryn. Mateo. Kai. Genevieve. Anya. Jude. Barrett. There are still others, whose names I have whispered while lighting candles or watching leaves fall from trees. The lengthening list breaks my heart, but the moms I have connected with continue to give me strength.

Two and a half years after Eliza was born, I met a few of these mamas in person. My friend Brandy generously opened her home near Chicago to a group of women she knew through blogs, emails, and social media, and we sent out an email call to Baby-Loss Mamas that we had gotten to know online, inviting them to stay in her home or in a hotel nearby.

We did not have any formal plans for this weekend in Chicago, but on Friday evening, we gathered in Brandy's house and we each got out the memory book or photo album or mementos of our babies that we had brought. We passed them around, shared them, and told or retold our stories. And we cried. I was crying not only for myself in that moment, but because I was in awe of these remarkable women whose babies had died and who were, somehow, not only living but making the most of their wild and precious lives.

As we talked, the stories I was hearing seemed unimaginable, and yet I kept reminding myself, not only were they real, they were also *my story*. I was living the "unimaginable" and here we all were together, grieving, but also talking and joking and connecting in a way that I had felt unable to do for so long.

And we laughed. It can be so hard to laugh at all after your baby dies. Like that moment when a laugh escaped me as I watched *Saturday Night Live* reruns, it feels almost wrong—like you're making light of something sacred or you're forgetting what should be the most significant thing on your mind. It feels like a betrayal because surely nothing in this life can be funny after you've held the silent bundle of a stillborn baby in your arms. But one of the most frustrating, funny, and beautiful things about this life is that it remains frustrating, funny, and beautiful, even when you're stumbling through a fog of grief.

The only time it feels safe to laugh—at least at first—is when you're with people who understand what that laughter means (and what it doesn't mean) because they have cried as long and as hard and as often as you have. They understand that laughter is not an indication of healing or recovery or improvement. It's not a sign that you're "better" or that you've "moved on," or that you are "back to normal." It's a recognition of the absurdity and humor of life that coexists with grief but does not cancel it out.

At one point, we were all cracking up about something Molly said and she remarked, "Just think how much fun I was BEFORE my baby died." And we laughed at that too, because it was dark and poignant and true. We are not the same people we'd been before our babies died, but we were with a group of people who had no expectation that we *would* be—and that in itself was a gift. Our group understood implicitly that the weight of grief shifted from one moment to the next, but it never left us entirely. We felt safe with each other, safe to joke and laugh, because we were with a group of people who knew that every moment of laughter had already been matched by twice as many moments of tears. We were with people who knew what it meant to love a "rainbow baby" with every ounce of delight and gratitude possible, and still to have a void in your heart that could never be filled. We were a group of people living with the ultimate disappointment and heartache—a reality that most people in first world countries never think about seriously—and yet here we were with a group of women who had suffered unimaginable loss and who were still full, complex, interesting, cute, and funny people.

When you are with other bereaved parents, especially those on a similar timeline, there's no need for context or justification. The differences that you have—religious, political, financial, geographical, philosophical—are diminished next to this enormous shared experience of babyloss. The only thing that made Eliza's loss tolerable was the group of women I found who were walking the same path. Wherever we gathered felt like a sacred space as I found myself with a circle of friends who knew and understood what it is to love and miss a child I don't get to hold in my arms. To say I am grateful for them is an understatement. That weekend was a healing balm on my heart, and those women were a marvelous gift to me. I still count them as some of my nearest and dearest.

CHAPTER 27

The spring after Eliza died, I rarely ventured out into the world unless I had to be somewhere (like work) or I was meeting a friend who had coaxed me to go out for coffee and who was unfazed if I cried in public. Most days, I could get up and go through the motions, but I still felt dangerously close to tears basically all the time. Day to day activities required an enormous amount of energy.

One unfairly beautiful day in April (I resented lovely spring days for a long time even while I appreciated the weather—how dare the world be enjoyable when I was miserable?), I went to lunch with a good friend of mine from grad school. Ben and I shared an office in the basement of the English department's building and we became friends as we commiserated over grading freshmen compositions and writing our dissertations. He was getting married in a few months, and I was happy to talk about wedding plans. My plan after lunch was to go to a quiet corner of the library with a stack of papers to grade, but Ben was on his way to visit one of the oldest cemeteries in St. Louis in preparation for taking one of his classes there on a field trip and he asked if I wanted to come along. It was Calvary Cemetery in North St. Louis, which contains the graves of some well-known people—Dred Scott, William Tecumseh Sherman, Kate Chopin, Tennessee Williams. Ben wanted to make sure he remembered where these graves were located so he could point them out to his students.

It was a glorious day to be outside, regardless of how much I resented the sunshine, plus grading is not my favorite activity, so it didn't take much convincing for me to accompany him. I think it helped that our destination was a cemetery. I felt a kind of solace surrounded by the markers of universal grief.

I hadn't been to a cemetery since Eliza died, and while my previous experiences had only been to visit the graves of my own grandparents or famous historical figures, I was now seeing everything differently as a new and bereaved parent. Everywhere I looked, I noticed children's headstones and empathized with the pain their parents must have felt.

William Tecumseh Sherman's grave has a miniature version next to it that marks the grave of his nine-year-old son: "Our Little Sergeant Willie."

Dred Scott's gravestone was covered in pennies, which pay homage to Lincoln freeing the slaves. I discovered that Dred Scott and his wife Harriet had a daughter named Eliza.

I saw another Eliza's name engraved on a stone in a lovely family plot. A stone near hers read, "Here lies Ann,

wife of Henry. Likewise their infant daughter Catharine."
The dates had worn away, but I thought it was safe to assume from the inscription that Ann and Catharine had died together. That was the moment I decided that someday my gravestone will also have Eliza's name on it, and I found a fragment of comfort in that idea. To make permanent the significance of a fleeting life—that's the purpose of these stones, isn't it? And in the great scope of things, aren't all our lives relatively fleeting?

After we had driven down to Kate Chopin's grave, Ben looked over the cemetery map and then asked if I wanted to go up to the Shrine of the Infants. My throat knotted up with unshed tears, so I nodded. And we walked up the grassy hillside.

It was heartbreaking to see these tiny baby graves on one big hilltop. Some of them with single dates, like my Eliza would have. Many of them with dates just days or weeks apart. Some of them with dates in the "wrong" order, for babies whose parents discovered their heart had stopped beating an entire twenty-four hours or more before their tiny bodies entered this world. The dates in this section were newer than many others that we'd seen in the cemetery—these started in the 1960s and went up to the present year. I didn't cry as I walked among the stones—maybe I felt a little self-conscious in front of Ben—but my throat felt swollen and my heart ached for those families, knowing too well the hopes and dreams buried on that hill.

As painful as it was to view these little headstones, it was also comforting in that it made me feel like one small part of something greater than my own hurt. My loss is so huge and all-encompassing, but a big cemetery full of strangers dating back for centuries is an undeniable reminder that we are all living one short chapter of a much larger narrative. And in that cemetery, I saw the staggering evidence of two hundred years of parents who have endured the loss of a child.

Ben and I didn't talk much as we walked around the infant shrine. When we got back in the car, he picked up the cemetery map again and spread it against the steering wheel so we could locate Tennessee Williams. To get there, we would drive by the Shrine of the Compassionate Mother—a large statue of the Virgin Mary.

Ben pointed at the map and said, almost like he was trying to lighten the mood, "Oh look. Shrine of the Compassionate Mother. That's you."

It was such an odd, off-hand comment. His said it with a smile, clearly something that had just popped into his head, and obviously, a bit of a joke (my habit of cursing and our tradition of beers at the local pub's trivia night didn't exactly inspire comparisons to the Virgin Mary), but the fact that he read the words "compassionate mother" and connected them to *me*, this no-longer-fun, no-longer-funny, always-on-the-verge-of-tears, mother without a child… it meant everything to me. We hadn't talked explicitly about Eliza that afternoon (mostly because that conversation topic reduced me to tears and I think we were both trying to avoid that) but, clearly, she had been on both of our minds.

Of all the nice things friends have said to me, that comment filled up my heart in a way I can hardly explain.

I think it was because he saw what was missing, where the biggest part of my heart had gone. He was also still hanging out with me, even though the qualities that I thought had made me fun (my sense of humor, sarcasm, and shared enjoyment of department gossip) had been flattened by my grief. We had shared an office as graduate students and we bonded over dissertation agony and teaching difficulties and crazy advisors and a love for literature and cheap Mexican food and beer and trivia, and now none of those things mattered to me anymore, but he was still showing up and seeing me for who I was. My pain scared me so much that I couldn't believe it didn't scare all my friends away. But here we were—wandering a cemetery. Talking about literature and looking at the graves of dead children and thinking about my daughter who was also dead.

It was astonishing to me that Ben could look past my grief and see me as a compassionate mother. I hadn't been able to put any other adjective with the word "mother" in regard to myself except for "bereaved." But I wanted his version to be true, too. Because Eliza made me *more* than just sad. She also made me open and aware and, yes, compassionate. I didn't know that anyone else could see that until I heard him say it out loud.

On that gorgeous spring day, four short months after I whispered good-bye to my precious baby girl, I still mostly felt that her loss had wrecked me entirely. I wasn't living the life I had wanted. My plans had been decimated, and I could have screamed for years about how unfair it was.

For a moment, driving past a huge statue of the Virgin Mary, Ben's Buick easing over potholes in the cemetery roads, it suddenly seemed possible that there was space for me to be something besides only and always a bereaved mother. Perhaps Eliza could also change my life in good ways, even without being here.

I smiled, but I didn't say anything in response to his comment. I guess I pondered it in my heart. (You know, like Mary, the original Compassionate Mother.)

Then we parked the car and approached Tennessee Williams's grave on foot, tucked away down a small, shady path. His epitaph reads: *The violets in the mountains have broken the rocks.* I took a deep breath and read those words again. Then, standing in front of the headstone, surrounded by shade trees and flowers, I began to weep silently. Not for Tennessee Williams (may he rest in peace), but because I was overwhelmed by the power of tiny, fragile, beautiful things—babies, flowers, whispers, tiny acts of kindness—and how they have the power to change the course of history.

Tiny flowers, tiny babies. Broken rocks, broken hearts.

I wept because I miss my baby girl more than I could ever say.

And I wept because I knew even then that loving her would make all the difference in my life.

It already has.

CHAPTER 28

I received a baby nightgown and blanket as a gift for Eliza from a dear family friend. The fabric was a soft yellow knit with white polka-dots and aqua-colored trim, and it was all packaged up in a sweet little decorative box with a baby duck on it. Above the duck were the words "Where did you come from, baby dear? Out of the everywhere into the here." I set the box up on a shelf in her room after my baby shower, near diaper cream and a soft baby hairbrush.

Eliza never wore that nightgown. But the rhyme on the decorative box kept circulating in my mind after Eliza died—almost like a chant I couldn't stop. She was *here*—she had been solid and real and moving and filling up my insides. Now, she was *gone*. But where did she come from? Where did she go? How did this happen? How could I get her back? How could the faith with which I'd been raised reconcile the abyss of grief with the promise of redemption? How could any promise of a future reunion make up for the miserable ache of loss that filled every waking moment? How could my faith withstand all my doubts and questions?

Even now, I cannot claim to have come to terms with my faith and my loss. I still have more questions than I have answers. I have more skepticism than I have trust. I have concluded that a life spent seeking answers to the important questions is a life well-spent. In my own search for answers, I have read Christian thinkers like C.S. Lewis and Jewish rabbis like Harold Kushner and Buddhist philosophers like Pema Chodron, as well as atheists and humanists. I have expanded my understanding of other faiths and focused less on what is correct and more on what is possible. I have come to terms with a sense of uncertainty, and in my best moments, I couple it with a vague hope for what might come next.

In truth, I still don't know how to feel about signs or winks, or the unknowingness of what comes after this life. A stanza from Tennyson's poem *In Memoriam*—a long poem about grief that I read in graduate school and revisited in my grief—comes to mind when I try to describe how I feel:

> *I stretch lame hands of faith, and grope,*
> *And gather dust and chaff, and call*
> *To what I feel is Lord of all,*
> *And faintly trust the larger hope.*

Faintly trusting "the larger hope" seems to be the best I can do, and I'm certainly not alone. It turns out that most poets who write about the grief of losing a child write about the painful uncertainty of their faith. The American poet James Russell Lowell wrote movingly about the death of his daughter, saying, "Console if you will, I can bear it: / 'Tis a well-meant alms of breath; / But not all the preaching since Adam / Has made Death other than Death." For people of faith, there is certainly a deep consolation in the prospect of being reunited, but even that cannot dispel the pain of earthly separation.

I'm not convinced that scarlet cardinal birds or fluttery butterflies or iridescent dragonflies or the improbably magical hummingbird are visitors from heaven. But every time I see one, I think of my girl. Is that so different?

Not long after Eliza died, someone sent me an article called "Why a Physicist Should Speak at Your Funeral." In it, Aaron Freeman explains, "You want the physicist to remind your sobbing mother about the first law of thermodynamics; that no energy is created in the universe and none is destroyed. You want your mother to know that all your energy, every vibration, every BTU of heat, every wave of every particle that was her beloved child remains with her in this world." I read these words and wailed, wanting the particles of my beloved child to line back up and form her perfect baby self. I made fists, gripping the empty air around me, wondering if I was clutching a particle of energy that had been part of her, shifted out into the everywhere. The reversal of the verse printed on that gift box. A letting go instead of a bundling up.

I have never visited a psychic or a medium to ask about Eliza. I'm a skeptic, I suppose, though if I'm being honest, it's mostly because I'm afraid of being disappointed. Recently, my friend Julie called me on her way home from seeing a medium, breathless about what she had been told. I listened, skeptical, as Julie related what the medium had said. He had told her that her daughter Anna, who died in December one year before my daughter, had a friend whose name began with E.

"E… Elizabeth?" he'd asked.

"Eliza?" she suggested.

The medium had nodded. Julie told me that right after that, he said that Anna was showing him a zebra. "Something about a zebra? Or the letter Z?"

Julie told him that Eliza's little sister is nicknamed Zuzu. The medium said that just as Anna is a guide and guardian for Julie's daughter Cate, Eliza is doing the same for Zuzu.

I was skeptical, but that didn't stop my heart from swelling at the thought.

Do I believe this? Can I trust it?

If I'm not sure, can I still allow it to bring me comfort?

The writer Doris Betts said, "I do not consider faith to be synonymous with certainty. Faith is the decision to keep your eyes open."

Mostly, I find myself sitting in uncertainty, keeping my eyes open, finding myself naturally skeptical, and trying to keep my heart open as well.

My husband was very close to his grandparents who had a huge role in raising him. It was an additional grief for us when his grandfather passed away about a year after Eliza. He never got to meet any of our children. At his grandfather's funeral, David delivered the eulogy and promised his grandfather that he would take care of his grandma, as he knew that his grandpa would be taking care of our baby girl. True to his word, when David's grandmother got cancer three years later, David was with her in her final days in hospice at her home. She talked frequently about her husband, Gene, and in her final days she would often reference him as though he were there and she was seeing him but couldn't talk to him. On a few separate occasions near the very end of her life, she would mention him as though he were in the room and she would say, "There's that little girl. He's holding that little girl's hand."

My wise friend Sarah—Otis's mom—says the veils are thin in these times of transition, which allows all sorts of magic and beauty to flow freely. Did David's grandmother see her husband and her great-granddaughter? Could it be that she saw my Eliza, three years later, holding her great-grandpa's hand? On the one hand, that seems impossible. On the other hand, who else could it be?

Do I believe it?

Can I allow it to bring me comfort even if I'm not sure?

The miracles of faith, of physics, of cellular biology, of life after death—these are all mysterious to me. As with all of us here on earth, I'm unable to fully understand or comprehend their intricacies and patterns. In this world, and the world beyond, there remain unknowns, unanswered questions, ideas about which no one can be completely certain, no matter how strong their faith.

I'm choosing to keep my eyes open. I rest in uncertainty. I acknowledge that mysteries exist beyond our comprehension, and maybe—just maybe—they swing toward hope. I acknowledge that her energy was real and was here and has not disappeared, though it has dispersed into the everywhere. And I find comfort when I imagine her now holding the hands of her great-grandparents on the other side of the stars.

Is that heaven? If those I love most will be there, how could it be anything else?

CHAPTER 29

Whatever we make of the afterlife, what doesn't change is the deep desire to parent our children on this side of the veil—to have the material, concrete experience of doing things with them and for them. Many of us, craving the ordinary tasks of parenting, turn toward other ways to remember and memorialize our children. We seek ways to honor them, excuses to say their names.

A good friend of mine attended a fundraising walk for childhood cancer after her niece was diagnosed with leukemia. She wrote later about the balloon ceremony, about the way the families were divided. Many families, including hers, had brightly colored balloons representing the children who were undergoing treatment or who had survived and were either in remission or living cancer-free. The white balloons indicated families in attendance whose children had died from cancer. My friend wondered how those families with the white balloons had the strength to be there. She wondered why they would want to continue to show up and raise money for medical research that hadn't happened in time to save their child, how they could bear to be there, to see other children who had survived when their beloved child had lost those odds.

What I didn't understand before becoming a bereaved parent myself is that sometimes showing up and holding a white balloon is a way to parent your child after she dies.

As parents, we have a fierce and undying desire to take care of our children. Living or dead, we want to parent them. And without the option of caring for a living child, we try to honor their memory in whatever way feels right to us.

We show up to a walk so that we can hear their names spoken aloud into a microphone at a park with a spotty sound system. We buy a t-shirt to see their names printed in tiny font on the back. We show up with our white balloons because our presence is a silent way to scream, "Her life still matters." We raise money and we make donations and we organize fundraisers and we run marathons and we lobby for legislation to allocate research money because we can't plan birthday parties or braid hair or hold a bike steady or drive them to piano lessons. We tattoo their names across our wrists, our shoulders, our backs because we want to make them visible. We donate books to libraries and diapers to diaper banks. We plant trees and we pay for bricks etched with their names and we put plaques on public benches. We do our best to create something permanent to mark the enormous significance of so brief a life.

This is not the parenting gig we signed up for, but it's the only one we've got left. So, when time and energy and funds allow, we do what we do in their names and in their memory. We honor them the only way we can. We show up and we hold the white balloons even when our hearts are bleeding and our teeth are clenched with the effort. We make them visible any way we can.

We honor our children in other, less public ways as well. We slip on a bracelet or fasten the clasp of a necklace engraved with their name. We decorate their gravestones for each holiday. We plant a memorial garden in our backyard. We include their name on a holiday card. We write their name in the sand. We frame their photo and hang it on the wall.

These moments are not always easy. There is an ache in each act of love. A great deal of time and energy is often required. Not all of us will build up blisters that turn to calluses as we train for a marathon to raise money for stillbirth research. Not all of us will be able to donate a hospital ultrasound machine or cuddle cot in memory of our child. Not all of us will be moved to show up and hold a white balloon. These are not proof of love—these are just some of the places love might go when we can't pour it into our living child.

But each time we find a new way to parent our child after their death, we are channeling our grief into something meaningful and doing our best to honor their memory.

The first year after Eliza's death, I did not attend the walk for remembrance that our local Share chapter organizes for grieving parents. It felt too hard, too sad. I didn't want to belong there. I also was afraid to invite friends and family who might not be able to attend. What would I do if I sent out an invitation and no one came?

The next year, I was determined to go. I didn't care if anyone else came with us. I felt like I needed to show up, to get Eliza's name printed on the back of the t-shirt. I sent out the invitation, sort of last-minute, to a couple of close friends who were local. Those friends kindly, apologetically replied that they had to work, or that they were out of town that weekend. No one could join us. We went anyway. We honored our girl by showing up, by hearing her name read aloud at a ceremony. We saw familiar faces—new friends from grief group—and we saw in every face the familiarity of grief, of loss, of determination. Now I'll occasionally see those t-shirts around town, and even though I'm a true introvert, I will always go out of my way to say: "I like your shirt. My daughter's name is on the back."

There is no right way or wrong way to honor a child who has died. Sometimes it means showing up for events that are specifically organized to recognize those we have loved and lost, and sometimes it means organizing those events ourselves, and sometimes it means we hold a quiet moment in our hearts. Often, though, it means showing up even when you have lost everything you hoped to hold. It's not to prove anything to anyone, it's when you have so much love to give, sometimes you need a place to put it.

I recently heard writer Elizabeth Gilbert suggest that after you've lost the only thing you've ever loved, the only thing to do is love everything. Perhaps the best and truest (and hardest) way to honor our babies is by taking the love we would have poured into them and doing our best to put that love out into the world.

PART FOUR

ONWARD

CHAPTER 30

Seven months after Eliza died, I went to Canada. I attended a work conference in Vancouver, and my whole family—my husband, and my parents and brother—decided to tag along to see a part of the world we hadn't visited before. Under normal circumstances, such a trip would have been thrilling. As it was, I could hardly muster interest in looking at guide books or vacation rental options to extend our stay. Vacationing while grieving is just crying in a new place, right?

A few days into our trip, I met up with a local Vancouver mom whom I'd been in touch with, first through my blog and then through email. We'd planned to meet at a coffee shop. I was so nervous. What if she was weird? What if it was awkward? What if we had nothing to say to each other?

She wasn't weird. It wasn't awkward. She wore jeans and a cute sweater and had a shiny ponytail and a wide smile. I was struck by how pretty and normal she looked, how anyone who saw us sitting at this little round table near the pastry display would think we were ordinary friends instead of mothers of dead babies. We sipped chai lattes and got teary as we talked about our babies, but we also laughed and it all felt amazingly normal. When we left, we hugged as though we'd known each other our entire lives.

It was life-giving. It was life-affirming. I hadn't yet worked up the courage to attend a grief support group so this was the first time I had sat with someone living my same grief on the same timeline and looked at her face and said, "Uh-huh. I know. Me too." And I got to hear those words echoed back at me. That encounter was one of the best things I'd done for myself since Eliza died. I left that coffee shop feeling a sense of hope that had been absent from my life for six months.

Of course, it didn't make the rest of the trip much easier. I wanted to appreciate this vacation, but the entire time we were in Vancouver, I couldn't stop thinking of how different things would be if Eliza were there, if we had a baby in tow everywhere we went. I wanted to be scheduling outings around nap time and carrying a bulky diaper bag everywhere. Instead, I walked unencumbered through farmers markets, browsed art galleries, visited breweries, went on hikes, and ate at restaurants, all with the pressure of unshed tears behind my eyes and tight in my throat.

After my conference wrapped up, we drove from Vancouver up in the mountains to Whistler. Everything about the ski resort town was gorgeous, even in July, and I tried to make the most of it, despite the weight of my unrelenting grief. We went white water rafting. We did more hiking. We visited more breweries. We sat in a hot tub and drank wine. And then we decided to go zip-lining.

It was a touristy thing to do—signing away our lives, strapping on helmets, walking up in the mountains, letting someone hook up harnesses to ropes so that we could swing suspended over trees and rocks and mountain streams. It's touristy for a reason—the view was breathtaking. Deep ravines, craggy peaks, evergreen trees silhouetted against impossibly blue sky.

As I stood on a man-made platform, surrounded by enormously tall trees stretching toward a sky that was as blue as I'd ever seen it, I felt a gift of peace. It wasn't exactly comfort, but it was a kind of acceptance, a weaving-in of Eliza's loss into my life. It was almost like I could see myself as a part of a greater scope, existing in a natural world that put out its offerings whether you took them or not, and was as indifferent to suffering as it was to joy. We call the death of a child *unnatural*, and it is in every way that matters, but such tragedies have been part of nature from the start. On this mountain, with trees and stones in sharp relief against an endless sky, I was aware of my own smallness in the vast universe. These trees had been here decades before me and they would continue when I was no more. These stones beneath my feet were eons in the making, and it occurred to me that the blip of my life should perhaps not be spent doubled over in grief, but reaching for whatever happiness I can grasp in these two hands.

I, who had been struggling for what felt like an age, who had spent an exhausting number of months raging against the irreversible and irrefutable, felt for a moment that maybe I could stop trying so hard and simply *be*. I took a deep breath, my lungs filling with the scent of cedar and the crisp mountain air. It was the first truly deep breath I'd taken in seven months. For the first time since Eliza's death, I felt new instead of old.

I know I'm not the only one to find a mysterious sense of peace by getting out into nature. The Japanese have a tradition called forest bathing. *Shonrin-yoku* is the idea that being among the trees can function as therapy. Health benefits, such as lowered heart rate and improved immune system function, have been scientifically proved. The phenomenon is not about exercise. Just *being* among trees is enough to change our bodies and our minds. Don't get me wrong—I didn't become one with nature and have some kind of revelation that caused me to go live alone at Walden Pond. I didn't stand on a mountain top and suddenly find internal peace. There was no easy fix. I had hoped to get pregnant on that trip, but I didn't. Instead, I stood among ancient trees on an ancient mountain, and I felt my own insignificance and the persistent throbbing of my heartbeat. I felt the enormity of our world and I felt alive to possibilities beyond this life. I felt the beauty of energy that cannot be destroyed or contained. I felt close to my baby girl, out of reach, but never far away.

With a carabiner clipped to a rope, I took another deep breath and swung myself out over an abyss. Held in the air by a manmade support of cords and pulleys, over a valley that plunged into shadow beneath me, I followed the example of our guide, flipping myself upside down and stretching out my arms. It was terrifying and exhilarating, and I felt completely resigned to whatever came next. The earth and sky reversed themselves; air rushed by my ears as I spun through space. I felt the adrenaline and the endorphins push the pain in my heart off to the side. I laughed out loud, giddy and breathless. And for a moment, for the first time in a long time, I felt like myself.

Everything in my life had been put on hold. For so long, I'd had the sensation of walking through quicksand, slogging along while every breath I took was saturated with grief. Time kept moving forward, but I was still looking back because I didn't want to turn away from Eliza. I didn't want to move on without my daughter. I assumed that the best of my life was behind me—I had achieved peak happiness during my pregnancy and I would never taste it again. I didn't want to exist in the present and I couldn't allow myself to imagine the future.

The mountain top gave me a new perspective on time. I saw so clearly that nothing human can last forever, not even the intensity of this grief. The world would go on spinning around me and instead of feeling offended and affronted by that, I felt myself begin to come to terms with it. I couldn't fast-forward myself through the pain, or find a way around it, but my grief muscles were strengthening so that I would be able to carry grief and put some of my attention elsewhere. I could integrate this loss and pain with other pieces of myself and my life. I might even be able to return to the person I had been—or at least to a recognizable version of that person. Undoubtedly, I would be changed. But perhaps not all that change would be detrimental. On top of a mountain in Whistler, Canada, I finally saw that the world was big enough for both pain and hope.

This was not an immediate cure for sorrow, but it felt like the first step forward. I can look at photos from that vacation—in which I'm smiling and even acting goofy—and I can see that I'm holding back tears. I can still feel the stranglehold of sorrow in my throat. But on a mountain, with a rope and a metal clip between me and a plunge into nothingness, I took a deep breath and jumped—headfirst—into that void. And I began to trust the secrets those old trees were whispering: that I could take a deep breath, step forward, and find beauty in this world again.

CHAPTER 31

I dropped off Facebook after Eliza was born. Deleted my account entirely. I had no place there anymore. Facebook was where I made joyful announcements. Bought a house! Adopted a puppy! Come to my PhD party! Guess what… we're expecting a baby!

To return to Facebook and post that my baby died felt impossible.

In 2011, Facebook had not yet become the hotbed of political vitriol and fake news, and other forms of social media were mostly nonexistent. I treated Facebook like a big, chatty dinner party. It was for small talk, witty observations, clever comments, socially acceptable life updates (or humble-brags), and occasionally maybe to get political. It was not a place to air my grief. In fact, I felt uncomfortable when people put their grief out there, and I could not imagine publicly airing my grief (except on my blog, which presumably someone would have to seek out intentionally). As I later told another babyloss mother, I could not bear the thought of anyone looking at Eliza's photographs who did not look at her with love.

When a former high school teacher of mine passed away a couple of years prior, I privately thought that the RIP messages on his Facebook page were strange and kind of morbid. I mean, it's not like he could *read* them. I didn't consider the comfort that they might offer to his family, or the way they allowed people to process his death. This was way back before Facebook had different emoji reactions available. There was no sad face or caring face, so I wasn't sure what to do when a friend from high school posted about missing his sister who had died from suicide. Should I "like" that post? What would I write as a comment? I scrolled on by.

(I want to go back and shake my old self and tell her, *Write "I'm sorry for your loss. Thinking of you." It's not that hard.*)

The problem was that I had been socialized by a culture that says we shouldn't talk about hard things—certainly not publicly. We are conditioned to think that grief is something to hide away, making it feel shameful. Society implies that it's our job to make sure we don't make other people feel bad or sad for us, no matter how bad or sad we're feeling. I saw these as the unwritten rules of social media, and so I no longer felt that I had a place there.

It didn't help that a few days after returning from the hospital, as I was logging in to shut down my account, I saw that the most recent post on my page was from a friend from graduate school who had recently moved to Pennsylvania. She was cheerily checking in on me and asking about my due date. How could I ever respond to that message on my Facebook timeline? How could I post a status update that said my daughter was dead? What would people do? What if they *liked* it? What if they *didn't*? How many of them would do as I had done before and scroll by, feeling awkward about it? I couldn't bear to find out.

I have come to know many families who used Facebook differently in the wake of their loss. There are incredibly supportive private groups on Facebook that can serve as online grief support. Some of my dear baby-loss mom friends formed a group called "Bitch, Please" in which they had a safe place to complain about all the terrible and hurtful and clueless and inappropriate things people said and did to them while they were grieving—ten years later, we still post there occasionally, on a variety of different topics. Many people I know relied on social media to get long distance communications and sympathy from friends and family members. It was a way to remind people that their baby was real and their loss was ongoing and unending. It can also offer an occasional gut punch—those "time hop" memory posts of where you were a year or five ago can feel like a kick in the teeth when they bring up the day you announced your pregnancy, posted "two weeks to go!" with your belly in profile, or included a photo of the nursery decorated for a child who never came home.

Facebook is like any other social media—it can be wonderful if you use it properly (and those in your network do, too). I couldn't do it. I didn't know how to navigate grief on Facebook and it felt too private, too personal, too risky to give it a try right after Eliza's death. I had to protect myself because any misstep would feel like an attack. I couldn't bear sentiments like "God needed another angel" or the dreaded "Everything happens for a reason." Even the old standard I had once recited myself: "I can't even imagine."

No. Nope. Absolutely not.

I knew that well-meaning and kind people were likely to say those things, and I knew that reading them would shred me, no matter how well-intentioned their words. I didn't have the energy to explain why I didn't want a guardian angel—I wanted my baby. If God wanted an angel and therefore took my baby from me, I wanted nothing to do with that God. If someone thought I was strong, it was because they didn't know me at all. If they thought this happened to me because I could *handle* it, then they had no idea how badly I was handling everything. And if they wanted to suggest that my daughter died *for a reason*—what kind of reason could possibly justify the death of a *child*? —I would want to kill them and see if they could figure out the *reason* I felt homicidal.

It was fear of the wrong reaction or a hurtful comment that made me step back from Facebook. Fear of people clicking away, of not caring. It was also the fear of me making other people uncomfortable. It was fear of being an object of pity. Fear of being reduced to "that girl whose baby died." Fear that I had been reduced to that already. There was an element of embarrassment, too, of shame that I had been unable to keep my baby alive.

I wanted to disappear. I couldn't disappear from my life, no matter how much I was hurting. So, I disappeared from my social media.

I kept blogging, though, even though it was public and out on the internet, because few people I knew in real life knew about my blog. It's no exaggeration to say that blog saved me. It was a place where I processed my feelings and pinned them down with words that I could control. It became a link to other bereaved mothers and a kind of shelter in my storm of grief. Whatever I was feeling, I could be confident that someone in the comments would say, "Me too." Those were the words I needed most to hear.

I stayed off Facebook for six years. I rejoined to be part of a couple of private groups for organizations I'd gotten involved with, but I began sharing a bit more of myself—including posts for Pregnancy and Infant Loss Awareness month in October, Eliza's birthday in December, and the complexities of Mother's Day when there are more children in your heart than in your arms. There is still a sting when posts I make about grief or Eliza get fewer comments or likes than other posts, but I have been pleasantly surprised that many people are willing to navigate the harder parts of life on social media. I have become more comfortable admitting my vulnerabilities online with people I know in real life. My life exploded when my daughter died and my desire to present a facade of perfection crumbled. There's no point in trying to cultivate a picture-perfect version of myself when my life is so obviously not perfect.

I have also noticed that even I have to *actively resist* scrolling past posts about other people's grief, posts that make me uncomfortable because they are not funny or pretty. I should not be surprised that so many people avoid commenting or "liking" or "sad-facing" a post about grief, because my first impulse is to scroll by it without engaging. It requires thought and energy, and sometimes I'm on social media scrolling mindlessly because I'm running low on those things. I also wonder if I'm overstepping when I comment on a loss of someone I don't know—an acquaintance from graduate school whose father died suddenly, but I'd never met the man. Or, perhaps it's weird for me to send a message to a girl I haven't seen since high school who posted that her mom died, when it's not like I knew her mother well.

Then I think about whether I would have appreciated a kind note from an acquaintance or an old classmate when Eliza died, and I send a message. It is usually quite simple: "I'm so sorry. I know how hard things must be right now. Thinking of you." Our losses are different, but I know grief. And I know how much it means for someone to say, "I understand" instead of "I can't imagine."

CHAPTER 32

Perhaps the most obvious expression of hope in the midst of grief was in our desire to have another child. Maybe the greatest show of hope that any bereaved parent can express is the decision to try again—to find a way to be a parent, even if is not the way we had originally planned. As great as my fear of another pregnancy loss was, my hope of having a family with living children was greater.

I knew immediately after Eliza died that I wanted to have another baby. Not because I thought it would ease the ache of missing her, but because I knew it was the only way to ease the ache of missing every part of parenting that we had looked forward to. It had taken us about six months of trying to get pregnant with Eliza. But I'd been thinking about and dreaming about her pregnancy for almost a year before that. I was finishing my graduate school, I was nearing the end of my twenties, many of my friends were getting pregnant or at least talking about it, and David and I were ready. I was ready to be a mom. I wanted to experience the biological miracle of pregnancy, of creating a baby with the person I loved most. I wanted to see who this baby would be and how she would be similar to or different from her dad and me.

I had not heard the term "rainbow baby" before I lost Eliza. The internet informed me that a rainbow baby was the child born after the storm of grief. I needed a rainbow in my life, because I could not see beyond the gray skies. It seemed clear to me that the only remedy for my broken heart was more love. If I couldn't have Eliza, I hoped we'd have the chance to have her sibling. Eliza was proof of the infinite measure of parental love, and more than anything else in this world, I wanted the opportunity to give that love to another child. My doctor felt that there was no reason we couldn't try again, and so we did.

There was a small part of me, a relentlessly optimistic piece, that thought we would get pregnant quickly because surely the universe would let *something* move in our favor. There was another part of me that feared I would be among those bereaved mothers who experienced secondary infertility, because, obviously, the universe was a destructive force intent only on bleak ruin, and why should I expect anything to ever work out in my favor? I knew both outcomes were very real and possible. I just didn't know which would be mine.

It didn't take long for it to become clear that I would *not* be one of those moms who gets pregnant immediately and has a baby close to the birthday of the child they lost. Instead, the weeks and months crept forward, and my longing only increased. I was desperately hoping to get a positive pregnancy test before the one year anniversary of Eliza's birthday. I wasn't sure how I would endure her birthday without being able to hold onto the hope of a new pregnancy. Every passing month felt like an added burden of grief, a shame-inducing slap in the face, and a relentless reminder of failure.

The struggle to get pregnant again was a struggle that David and I kept private for the most part. I shared what was happening—or not happening—only with fellow loss-mamas. I couldn't bear the encouragement or pity of anyone else. Each month felt like a small-scale tragedy, as I feared my loss would be compounded by unexplained secondary infertility. The number of months it took to get to that diagnosis hardly mattered—I felt it in my bones. I felt like a failure.

It didn't matter that my identity went beyond motherhood. It didn't matter that I knew women could have big and fulfilling and delightful lives without having children. What mattered is that I wanted a baby. I had a baby. My baby died. I wanted her back. I wanted a baby to hold. I wanted to fill this desperate longing. I wanted to be pregnant again. I could not escape this reality, no matter how much I knew that I had a valuable life apart from motherhood.

I had a loving family, a devoted husband, supportive friends, a good job, a nice home, a great life. Logically, rationally, I knew that I wanted to cultivate an identity and a life for myself outside of being a mom. But also? I wanted to be a mom. And now that my baby was dead, I felt like nothing else mattered.

As each month left me as bereft and childless as the

month before, despite my absolute belief that a woman does not need children to feel complete, happy, and fulfilled, I felt the opposite of all those things. I was miserable and desperate. I felt like a medieval queen whose relationship, reputation, and survival depended upon her producing an heir.

This pressure was self-imposed. Certainly, David wanted another baby, too, but he wasn't blaming me. I knew my parents had been delighted with the idea of a grandchild, but my mom had specifically written to me (probably in response to my suffering) that it was perfectly fine if Eliza was their only grandchild. I was so grateful for that note and it made me cry so hard. I knew how excited my mom had been. I wasn't sure I believed her, but it did take some of the pressure off me. Not only was I wanting the chance to be a mom again, I also wanted to give my parents a grandchild and couldn't quite let go of that feeling that I had failed them, too.

I kept lying to people, insisting that we weren't ready to try again because I couldn't bear to hear encouragement or see pity in their eyes. One of my best friends blurted out six months into my grief, "I thought you would be pregnant again by now." All I could do in response to that was cry, and she later apologized profusely. But what I was thinking at that time was, "Oh, my God. Me too." It felt like I would be stuck in my grief until a new pregnancy gave me forward momentum. I'd gotten to know other women who had losses around the same time I did, and it seemed like they were all getting pregnant again. I felt panicky about being left behind, wallowing in my grief alone, left sinking in quicksand while the others stumbled forward without me.

After six unsuccessful months of trying, I was unwilling to wait any longer. I made an appointment with a reproductive endocrinologist who monitored my cycle to determine treatment. He was kind and sympathetic as I sobbed my way through our first appointment. After I'd made another office visit for the scheduled scans and ultrasounds, we met to discuss the plan for my next cycle. He was pleased because, as he explained it, my problem wasn't any of my reproductive organs. My ovaries were creating and growing the follicles properly to produce an egg, my tubes were clear, and my uterus was healthy. But my brain wasn't giving the signal to my body to release the egg. He was optimistic that all I needed was a trigger shot to tell my body to ovulate.

The doctor obviously felt this was good news—and clearly it was. I knew that I was lucky not to require an expensive or invasive procedure. Ideally, a little hormone boost would get things moving. The doctor looked somewhat baffled when I burst into tears immediately upon hearing this news. Perhaps thinking I had misunderstood him, he started to painstakingly explain the test results again.

Intellectually, I knew this was good. Emotionally, I couldn't help but feel angry and guilty. It wasn't my body that was preventing me from having a baby. *It was my brain.* I couldn't get out of my own way. Maybe it was grief? Maybe it was anxiety? Maybe it was my unconscious brain's way of punishing me for not keeping Eliza safe?

Whatever my brain chemicals were doing, my heart wanted another baby, and I was ready to walk on hot coals, or, in this case, spend a lot of money on needles at the local pharmacy, to make it happen. It just so happens that I have always had a needle phobia. It started when I fainted while getting a flu shot when I was in high school. In college, I passed out while donating blood. I had to have my wisdom teeth removed when I was in my twenties and I fainted dead away *while sitting reclined in the chair*, already wearing the paper bib, simply because I looked over at the long row of needles lined up on the counter.

But this doctor sent me home with a prescription for lots of needles. There was a series of tiny injections for my tummy to boost follicle production and then a trigger shot that David needed to administer in my butt cheek on a specific day of my cycle to make me ovulate. My issue with needles has never been the pain *or* the puncture. I didn't shy away from acupuncture and I have a pretty high pain tolerance. It's a mental thing, the notion of some substance oozing into me (or being removed from my veins). It makes me feel a little light headed even to write about it in this moment.

But these needles? These shots? My focus was on the goal, and I felt in that moment that I would have shoved needles under my fingernails if I could have gotten pregnant that way. As far as I was concerned, the end would justify any means necessary. I relished the ritual of turning on the television, icing my abdomen to numb the skin, and stabbing myself with a tiny needle every day.

I got a strange satisfaction from the dot of blood that would sometimes well up. I was more than willing to work for a baby, as though I could earn another chance.

If life were a meritocracy, I thought, I could have *earned* a baby by now. I would have been happy to follow a regimented diet, keep to a specific exercise regimen, study for any test necessary, jump through literal or figurative hoops to bring home a baby. And, frankly, I was irritated that most women in this world got to bring home babies without doing any of that work.

But instead of being promised a baby as reward for a demonstration of my dedication and hard work, I was told to go have sex, promised that I had a 20% chance of getting pregnant each month. The odds did not seem to be in my favor. The small measure of control that I felt when I stabbed a slender steel tube into my flesh was worth the discomfort. I felt like I could handle anything if I could just get a baby in the end. Knowing all along that even if I did get pregnant again, a living child was not guaranteed was more terrifying than the needles themselves.

I got pregnant the second month we did the needles and the trigger shot, much to the delight of the nurses at the RE's office. My response to those two lines on the pregnancy test was so different than what it had been before. Instead of celebrating, my shoulders sagged under the weight of what would come next. What had felt like peak excitement last time now felt like the first rung of a very high, very steep ladder that I would be clinging to for the next nine months. I had been longing to get pregnant, but there was no satisfaction in having that longing fulfilled. The desire for another pregnancy was completely overshadowed by my longing for a healthy, living child and the underlying anxiety about how to make that happen. My desire for another child felt as powerful and uncertain as my longing for pregnancy had been in the moments before the test results. This was no time for a giddy reveal to David. This was the first step of a journey that required white knuckles and gritted teeth. All I wanted was to hold my own living, breathing baby in my arms. I just couldn't trust that it would happen.

It did happen. Eighteen months after we lost Eliza, we had another baby girl. I held a squirming, squalling, still-slippery baby in my arms and cried with joy and relief. She was alive. I had another chance to parent a little girl. I got to take her home and soak up every moment of her—it was all I had dreamed about, and I had hardly let myself believe it would happen. I hadn't unpacked any little clothes or baby things. I didn't set up a nursery. I didn't buy diapers. All those things could be done after she arrived. Instead, I counted kicks and recorded them obsessively. I went to appointments for non-stress tests and biophysical profile ultrasounds. I saw my doctor weekly in the third trimester. David fell asleep each night with his hand on my stomach, feeling her kick and move under my taut skin.

Eighteen months after Eliza died, her younger sister was born. It is no exaggeration to say that it was the happiest day of my life. As Kahlil Gibran says, "Your joy is your sorrow unmasked" and I'm not sure I'd ever understood that line until I had a living baby after having birthed a dead one.

I kept thinking of the term "rainbow baby" as I held Eliza's sister. Eliza died on a cold, black December night. A year and a half later, I held my rainbow baby in my arms on a sunny afternoon in June and I marveled at my good luck. Despite all that I had lost, I now recognized the luck and the privilege that allowed me to get this baby earthside and alive. I was grateful for quality health care, for a doctor who cared about me, for having had the financial means to pursue reproductive technology. I grieved for women who did not have that same access or opportunity. And I knew that those things, as necessary as they were, were not enough to guarantee me this miracle swaddled in my arms.

But rainbows can shine even when the rain continues. Grief does not evaporate, but it does shift and change. Sometimes there is barely a cloud in the sky. Other times it can feel like it's pouring even after the rainbow is here.

We named our second daughter Caroline Audrey. We gasped at her cuteness and marveled at her softness and giggled at her squeaky newborn noises. The nurses celebrated with us and my doctor joked with us and my parents went to our house to wash a load of little pink pajamas. I sat in the hospital bed, facing a big window of blue sky and sunshine and I made a few promises to myself, to Eliza, and to her little sister. I promised that Eliza would not be our family's scary secret—that we would talk openly and honestly about our loss and grief and about the joy that followed. I promised that I would do all I could not to parent out of fear. I knew that the death of one child would undoubtedly influence how I raised our other children, but I wanted to be sure that their lives would not be limited or encroached upon by my anxieties, at least to the best of my ability. And I promised to love this baby for who she was—not a replacement for Eliza, but a beautiful baby girl in her own right who was here in this world not because Eliza had died, but because in her brief life she showed us how much we wanted to be parents.

In the years that have passed since Eliza died, we have gone on to have three living children. I never expected to be pregnant four times. I never dreamed that all four of my babies would be girls. It makes me feel like a mother in a Jane Austen novel. I continue to marvel at my good fortune and am amazed that it is possible that I have a dead baby and I still consider myself "lucky." To this day, I am astonished that I have three living children and while I am far from a perfect parent, I do not take their existence for granted.

I've discovered that motherhood is rarely as straightforward a proposition as I had assumed it would be. The path to get there is often long, winding, full of obstacles, or ultimately takes us someplace different altogether. I have gotten to know a few other women who lost babies and were unable to have children afterward. While I admit that this prospect terrified me at the early stages of my grief, I have now seen the way these women move in the world, finding their way through grief and infertility to grit, grace, and humor. I've seen their recovery take time, as they were forced to grapple with the circumstances of childlessness not by choice in addition to their grief, but they have been examples to me of the identity and value we all have beyond our role as mothers, and of the way that life is not "ruined" even when it is completely different from what we had once hoped and expected.

I also know and love many women who are childless by choice or by circumstances other than loss, and they model the kind of life I know I could eventually have found fulfilling. I've connected with several women who became mothers in unconventional ways—through fostering, adopting, egg or sperm donation. What we all have in common is a willingness to eventually come to terms with life as it is rather than life as we had dreamed. We may come at it grudgingly, and it is a hard-won triumph for most of us, but all the bereaved mothers that I have known eventually find the ability to love life again, no matter how impossible that notion once seemed.

CHAPTER 33

As much as I wanted another baby, I struggled with the idea of "moving on" or "accepting" our loss. Even before Eliza died, I was aware that acceptance was considered the last of the five stages of grief. I was also vaguely aware that those five stages had sort of been declared bunk—or at least therapists and psychologists recognized that grief is not progressive and linear, so these stages do not proceed in a neat, orderly manner. Depression, anger, denial, and bargaining were all part of the package, though their order was not predictable. The idea of acceptance made me clench my fists and tighten my jaw—the death of my daughter was not something I could simply accept and put behind me as I moved on with the rest of my life.

I became familiar with other parents who referred to life after loss as their "new normal." That phrase also made me clench my teeth. There was nothing *normal* about this. Not only was it completely abnormal and unnatural for me to leave the hospital empty handed, I couldn't stand the idea that this feeling of helpless, nauseating misery was now the status quo of my life. I needed this to be an aberration, a mistake that could be corrected, a terrible detour with time for us to still get back on track. I didn't want a *new normal* in which grief and loss was a permanent part of my life. I wanted my old normal. The one where I was happy.

My first desperate thought when I was told my baby had no heartbeat was that I wanted to call for a do-over. I was in agony from contractions, but it was the news of her death that made my insides twist up, waves of horror and nausea that made me vomit. And even as I sobbed the word "No," and retched and puked and squeezed my eyes shut and shook my head, I wanted to time travel. I wanted to go back and fix this. I wanted everything to go back to the way it had been just a few moments, hours, days before. I was still madly in love with my former life. Months after her passing, I still couldn't quite shake this desire and I sobbed to David, "I don't want this life! I want the life we were *supposed* to have!"

In fact, the permanence of the situation, with no end to my grief, and no way to change it or fix it or make it better—that was part of the horror. And maybe I could acknowledge this truth, but I didn't want to *accept* it. I didn't want to fold it into my experience and then continue to go on without her. No matter what came next, no matter what good fortune might befall me, the unchangeable fact of her death would always be there. Early on, I understood this to mean that my life was ruined. It sounds dramatic, perhaps, but her loss cast such an enormous shadow, I couldn't see myself ever coming out from under it. My first child would *always* be dead, and I would *always* be devastated by that fact. How could everything that came after not be ruined? She would never not be dead, and I would never not be missing her. My future was an emotional black hole. I couldn't fathom what it would mean for this to "get easier" or for me to "feel better."

What could better possibly look like when these circumstances would never change? How could I ever find peace, come to terms with this, or accept that this was my life? I could grimly accept the reality that my life would somehow go on, but it seemed clear that my remaining time on the earth would be infected by grief. Any good thing that might follow must always feel shadowed or diminished by the weight of this loss. How could I accept that this daughter, whom we'd named, celebrated, and fully expected to raise, would never take a breath or open her eyes? How could I accept the ongoing overwhelm of disappointment in the form of an ache so deep I couldn't see my way out? How could I accept that this was my reality forever and still want to go on living?

But when the path divides like that, the split between the old life and the new, forever marked by something tragic, there's no do-over. We can't double back and try again. We can move forward or we can stand still. We can wish with all our might, but then we must wake up to the world around us. I learned that acceptance doesn't mean that we stop wishing things could be different. Acceptance isn't the same as approval. My therapist told me another way of thinking about it is integrating grief into your life without letting it swallow up everything. Grief gets threaded through everything because love is threaded through everything, but integrating the loss into your reality is accepting that you can't change things, while also honoring your baby and carrying her memory forward. At some point, I stopped spending all my energy on wishing for a different life and I started doing what I could to make the reality of this life manageable and—someday—even enjoyable.

In the early days, that lesson was wasted on me. I lived and breathed my grief and it was all-consuming. As the months went by, I made a conscious effort to appreciate the good that came my way. It will never be good *enough*. It will never make up for what's been lost. But we all know that life can be terribly, horrifically, unbelievably awful. So, if something small—clean sheets on a freshly made bed, a bowl of chili and a bottle of hard cider, a long walk with a happy dog—gives me a reprieve from the sadness, I'll take it. And I won't feel bad about it, or guilty that I'm somehow being disloyal to her memory, because I know that no matter what happens, I'll never, ever in a million years have enough joy to make up for the sadness of Eliza's death. Even so, that doesn't mean I can't have any happiness at all.

At first, though, I didn't know how to come to terms with a life that seemed doomed to be nothing but disappointment. Moving forward in a new reality meant accepting that disappointment as a fact of my life while also believing that this tragedy wouldn't encompass my entire existence forever. It meant accepting that there was more life beyond and in addition to my grief. Still, I dreaded moving forward because it seemed to suggest that I was moving *away* from Eliza. I held tight to my grief because I was afraid that if I loosened my grip on my sorrow, I would be letting go of my baby. I came to realize that I cannot leave behind what is a part of me. Loving her and losing her are inextricable to who I am today—as a person, as a mother. She has shaped me more profoundly than any other life experience. In one way or another, nearly everything I do and everything I feel traces a line back to her.

You might have heard that Leonard Cohen quote, "There is a crack in everything. That's how the light gets in." It seemed clear to me that the great crack in my life was the irreparable loss of my daughter. But I didn't know how much she would continue to be a part of my life in ways that weren't merely sad and miserable. My life would always be marked and shaped by this tragedy, but the scars didn't have to signify ruin. It was possible for my life to be marked and shaped by my love for Eliza, and not my grief alone.

Acceptance does not have to mean thinking that everything happened for a reason, or this was somehow meant to be, or that life is working out according to some greater plan. While some may find comfort in those ideas, I do not subscribe to that line of thinking. I can make Eliza's life and death meaningful by what I choose to do with my own life, and I can do my best to live in a way that honors her, but the death of a child holds no moral lesson for me or anyone else, as far as I'm concerned. I have zero interest in a divine plan that includes the cruel sacrifice of innocents, and I cannot believe in a loving God who operates in that method.

What I can accept, though, is that this is the way my life has unfolded. All I can do now is to find a way to honor my baby by creating meaning from the truth I cannot deny. I needed to do this to survive. Acceptance came for me when I acknowledged that moving forward was not the same as letting go. Early in my grief, I read a piece of writing on the *Glow in the Woods* website, and I copied down the words, not yet trusting in their truth. Another mother, a woman named Branwen, whose life was marked by grief like mine, had started a new job and was reflecting on what this meant for her relationship with her (dead) daughter: "My heart panics, but when it catches up with reality, everything becomes clear: she is still with me, she is still gone. No more, no less. Wherever I put my heart and my energy now, it is because of her and what she has made me. She can't possibly be left behind."

I read that passage with a breathless hope a few months into my grief. Now I've been here long enough to know that it is true.

Other baby loss mothers promised me that it wouldn't get better but it would get easier, and I didn't quite understand what that meant, either. But they were right. As time went on, I got more comfortable carrying the burden of grief, and—most amazing—I reached a point where it didn't feel like so much of a burden as a connection, a link, an opening—a crack where the light could get in.

When I consider my dear friends and acquaintances whose lives are also marked by loss, and whose trajectories mirror my timeline of grief, I can see all the ways they make meaning of grief by shaping it into love. All of them have moved forward. Their lives are full, and contain more than sadness. Not one of them has forgotten their grief or left their child behind. Some of them have gone on to have more children. A few remain childless by circumstances outside of their control. Some of them lead grief support groups. Some of them practice random acts of kindness in honor of the child they lost. Some of them have organized amazing fundraisers—5K races, trivia nights, and other events—and they donate that money to research to prevent stillbirth or to grief support for bereaved families. Some of them train for and participate in marathons and donate their sponsorship money to medical research. Some of them foster children whose biological parents are unable to care for them. Some of them mark their child's birthday by requesting diaper bank donations, or school library donations, or other charitable acts that are meaningful to them. All of this adds up to enormous good that is going back into the world, and all of this is done in honor and memory of children who are loved and wanted and no longer with us. I can see now that this is a form of acceptance as well as a fierce will to do good in their names—to carry our grief forward as we also carry on with love.

I remember, too, how impossible it felt to do anything meaningful or good while crushed by the weight of early grief. As Eliza's first birthday approached, I felt paralyzed and inadequate. Not only had I not done fundraising or started a nonprofit or trained for a marathon, I had no energy to tackle any of those things and no idea how I could possibly commemorate her birthday in a way that would be meaningful to me and feel like it was doing her justice. I just wanted my baby back. I didn't want to do something nice in her memory.

CHAPTER 34

Before Eliza died, I had no idea how many people were grieving. I did not realize how much the act of being human requires us to walk around looking normal on the outside while feeling shattered on the inside. I did not fully understand how resilient we can be—how resilient I could be. I did not know that I could be broken and still function, that I could be broken without being destroyed.

The Japanese art of Kintsugi is the repair of broken objects with a special lacquer mixed with gold. Instead of trying to hide the fracture lines, the broken places in the pottery are highlighted with gold. In the end, the real beauty of the ceramic piece comes from its cracks and flaws, where the gold shines in the broken places and the whole piece becomes something different and more beautiful.

The Canadian singer Lhasa de Sela writes about having your heart broken—not broken into pieces, but cracked wide open. I remember reading an essay by Kate Inglis, another bereaved mother and a remarkable writer, about her thoughts on these lyrics at the website *Glow in the Woods*. The world felt so dark and ugly to me, but here was a grieving mother who seemed to glimpse a golden thread in this grief. Not a silver lining or a crappy consolation prize, but beauty that emerges from brokenness.

That's the beauty and the pain of it, isn't it? That love remains when life is gone. This power to go on loving is what makes us human and fragile and vulnerable and it's also what makes us fierce, invincible, immortal.

I am deeply moved by this idea that once we love someone, that love does not die with them. Love never leaves. Eliza died, but the love she brought into our lives remains—even if it hurts for a long while. Love came here, and here it stays. It's the simplest and loveliest way I can think of to describe Eliza's life.

Could my heart be open—no longer closed off or crumbled into dust, despite having been shattered into a million pieces? Would I someday be able to face the world unafraid?

The truth is there are days when I feel that my loss has strengthened me and equipped me to face any hardship with resilience and fortitude. After all, I've survived worse. To know we have everything to lose, that crushing grief is just a heartbeat away, and to choose love anyway? It's the whole point of being here and being human.

Eliza showed me that when we love we always risk loss, and love is worth that risk.

There were also days when my grief felt like such a burden that I wasn't sure I could face another challenge or obstacle, no matter how small. But even while my heart was at its most raw, torn, and exposed, it also opened me to conversations and community I'd never experienced before. Eliza's life revealed to me the grief in our midst. The invisible suffering I'd never noticed before was suddenly a solid object, and one that I realized many, many people were carrying.

It turned out that some of the most beautiful people I knew got that way because they had survived trauma, loss, illness, or grief in some measure. We were all broken. We just had to let our light shine through the broken places. Sometimes I would think that I had to do this for Eliza, that it was too much responsibility for a baby to know that she'd broken her mother's heart. I had to be okay for her—I still didn't want to think of her worried or sad.

Facing a lifetime without my daughter felt like a punishment, but I can see some of the ways in which my life after Eliza has also been full of gifts. From the beginning, my pregnancy was a gift with many strings attached—falling in love with someone whose life can slip away is a dangerous proposition. But who hasn't done this? And where would we be without this love? I'm not convinced that there is anyone in this world who isn't a little bit broken, or who won't be broken at some point in the not-so-distant future. It's the price we pay for being human and loving well.

My grief for Eliza most days is no longer the heart-shattering, chest-sinking, throat-closing agony that it was at first. It's now less of a heart-break and more of a heart-ache. Heartache feels a lot like homesick. It's that a nostalgic feeling that makes your chest tight but doesn't quite bring you to tears. It makes you want to stop talking though, it makes you have to maybe catch your breath or you realize much later you've been clenching your jaw. It's a tired kind of ache. It's not a slicing, searing pain. It's a push on a tender place. These days, my grief is not the nauseating, breathtaking agony it was. It's a throb of longing and a wistful consideration of what might have been.

It took a long, long time to be able to feel that I could enjoy my life again, that I could do so without betraying my daughter who didn't get to live this life. Loving life comes easier now, my grief rests lighter. But I still have moments when that familiar ache rises up and I get that bubble of unshed tears in the back of my throat. The difference is that the heartache feels less like it is ruining my life and more like it is enriching it, reminding me of my first girl.

It's the feeling I get when I come across someone else named Eliza. It's a fairly uncommon name, so I don't hear it often. I feel possessive of Eliza's name. It's not reasonable. After all, it doesn't bother me to meet other children who share names with my living children. But it makes my heart ache to hear someone else saying Eliza and taking it for granted. I miss getting the chance to write it on forms and name tags and backpacks. I still wish I were labeling things in Sharpie with her name or ordering a monogram of her initials. I miss her name on all the accoutrements of childhood. I talk about Eliza, but when I consider the number of times I've said my living children's names compared to the number of times I've said her name… it's not even close.

I love all my girls' names, but Eliza is still my favorite name. I like that it's short to spell but still musical to say. Somehow sounding both modern and old-fashioned. A nod to Jane Austen novels, a romantic three-syllables, but stately enough for a future appointment to the Supreme Court. In my mind, it's the perfect name. I'm envious of those who get to say it every day, multiple times a day, particularly if they're directing it toward a little girl they love.

Heartache is getting together with friends and seeing their four children born within three months of Eliza. Heartache is that group photo of all the cousins—all except for one. I adore my niece and nephew, and I feel joyful when we are all together, but that joy exists alongside the heartache—a bittersweet combination.

My heart aches when I wonder whether anyone else is thinking about her and when my husband squeezes my hand so I know that he is. It aches when I wonder whether anyone else recognizes that empty space in the photograph where she would fit right in. It is such a gift when someone else points out her space (usually another bereaved parent seeing the picture on social media). Heartache is missing her at every milestone, even while I can celebrate them again. Heartache is being able to smile and laugh and enjoy such moments as back to school photos and Halloween costumes (*finally*—it was a long, hard slog), but also feeling the longing for her in every single one.

Heartache is different than that sharp, wild grief of early loss. These days, heartache can nearly crescendo without bringing me to my knees. Heartache is when a child's voice asks from the backseat of the car, completely out of the blue, "Mommy, why did Eliza's heart stop beeping?" and I can answer her in calm measured tones, and say that we just don't know.

Heartache is the quiet but persistent reminder that someone is always missing. Our family may look complete, but I'll always ache for what I might have been, and what our family might have been if Eliza were here. Heartache is love turned into eternal longing. Life is sweet again, but my heart will always ache for my first baby girl.

CHAPTER 35

I remember how impossible it felt to do anything meaningful or good while crushed by the weight of early grief. I am now approaching my tenth year without my first girl, and this grief has grown familiar. No longer a monster breaking down my door, it's familiar and I prepare for it, trying to take care of myself the way I would if I were physically ill. I clear my calendar, I plan to get take out dinner, I take off work and let myself spend the day curled up on the couch. I miss her, but I have built a life around that missing piece, holding space for her, carrying the weight of her grief the same way I carry the weight of my toddler up the stairs—a bit tilted, perhaps, but steady on my feet.

The first year without her was undoubtedly the hardest. My grief was physical, palpable, a force I could not control. As Eliza's first birthday approached, I felt paralyzed and inadequate. I was in awe of bereaved parents who were doing great things in memory of their children. Not only had I not done fundraising or started a nonprofit or trained for a marathon, I had no energy to tackle any of those things. When I thought about her birthday, I felt like I was suffering from the flu. I was heavy, lethargic, chilled and shaky. Nothing I did would be good enough or big enough, and I couldn't bear to fail her by doing something mediocre.

I was determined, though, that her birthday would not be ignored. I ordered greeting cards to send to close friends and family. On the front of the card, I had printed a photograph of a beach sunset with her name written in the sand. On the inside, I had printed the following:

In loving memory of
Eliza Taylor Duckworth
December 6, 2010

Please join us in remembering
our sweet Baby Duck
on the anniversary of her birthday.

Though we cannot hold her in our arms,
we carry her always in our hearts.

Then, in smaller font at the bottom, I added:

Thank you for the love and support we've been given in the past year. The sorrow we feel for our daughter's loss can only be matched by the love she brought into our lives.

You are invited to join us in celebrating Eliza's brief but beautiful life by lighting a candle, by sharing a moment of silence, or by performing an act of kindness in her honor.

We'd love it if you would share with us how you choose to remember her.

I needed to do this, because I wanted to make sure that people knew we wanted them not only to remember Eliza, but to talk to us about her. I knew from my own mistakes and missteps how hard it can be to mention someone who has died for fear of upsetting someone else. I wanted to be sure to give people permission to say her name to us.

Eliza's birthday happens to be the same day that the Share organization holds a candlelight vigil for bereaved families who have lost children, so that is what we did. We showed up and we held a candle and I cried through the brief outdoor service in the winter wind and it was both enough to get me through the day and completely insufficient. Now it's our standing plan to go every year. Many of my friends who have lost a child find comfort in creating a tradition to follow, whether it's a butterfly release, a picnic under a tree, a candle lit at the dinner table, a donation made in memory of the child. There's a relief in deciding once and letting that tradition stand. The act itself matters less than the ritual.

We have come to incorporate the tradition of the candlelight vigil into our annual acknowledgment of Eliza's birthday. In my mind, I always envision carefully choosing the perfect white flowers to leave at the base of the angel statue, eating together as a family at a restaurant, where our children are somber and well-behaved, and then all of us experiencing the vigil as a solemn and spiritual occasion, during which my feet do not turn numb from the cold and my children do not knock over luminaries.

In real life, there have been years when I found myself grabbing a bouquet of flowers at the grocery store, years when we've grabbed fast food so that we wouldn't be late to the ceremony, and a couple of times we've ducked out of the ceremony early because my children were misbehaving or it was so cold I literally lost feeling in my toes.

The execution of the day may never match the vision in my mind, and nothing could never measure up to what I had wanted that day to be, but what's important to me now is the ritual. This is what we do. It doesn't have to be perfect—it just has to be a small space we hold for her. Some years will be better than others, but we honor her by showing up. By creating a family tradition that becomes part of the fabric of our lives, and that holds Eliza's place in our family.

I think one of the greatest gifts David gave me was turning to me to say, "What do you want her birthday to look like this year?" This gave me the space to explain that I wanted to mostly just lie on the couch. I wanted a fancy dessert, but I didn't want to make it. I wanted a candle lit, but if I'd left all of that for the day of, I might not have had the energy to make it happen. We worked together to organize it in advance, and we kept our expectations low. Marking the worst day of my life, while highlighting the love I feel for Eliza is a tricky balancing act, and one I never do as well as I'd like.

Incorporating the heartbreaking truth of loss into your life allows you to find a way to honor your baby's memory by making space for it—first amid the deluge of heavy grief in the early days and then in the hustle and bustle of life years later. It means prioritizing that memory above all other things, even for a moment. This doesn't only have to happen annually on your baby's birthday—it can be a daily prayer or meditation, a seasonal visit to the cemetery, a candle lit on holidays, incorporating an object in memory of your baby into future family photos, or a random act of kindness that only you will know was in memory of your child. It might mean posting actively on social media during October's Pregnancy and Infant Loss Awareness month, or putting up the same picture on your social media each year on your child's birthday. It doesn't have to be the same thing each year, either, but finding a ritual and a routine has helped me bring Eliza into our family's traditions in a way that feels meaningful and doesn't overwhelm me with the need to make a bunch of decisions around the anniversary of her birth and death, when I'm struggling the most with grief.

What I think "acceptance" means is not exactly

making peace with your loss, but is taking that emptiness and moving forward with it. You can honor your baby by letting their death—and their brief life—give your life purpose and direction, to feel and acknowledge the pain and the joy of unconditional love, and to be gentle with yourself when you feel that nothing you do could be enough.

Once we have incorporated our greatest loss into the life that follows, then we have room to *do* something in the emptiness that is left behind, whether that action is a public display or a private moment at home. No ritual will ever be enough to represent adequately the significance of your child and his or her brief life. Nevertheless, we honor our babies as we carry their memories, as we allow grief and love to be our teachers, as we carry forward with ordinary activities and new family traditions.

CHAPTER 36

It's a relief for me to be certain that I am done having babies. I have four daughters: one dead, three living. I will not have any more children. To have the anxiety and fears of pregnancy behind me has felt like closing the door and leaving behind a room that I have no desire to revisit. I am not someone who rests comfortably in uncertainty. I feel better once a decision has been made or an outcome is absolute.

To rest in uncertainty is to recognize the fleetingness of life, of any given moment. This does not feel restful. Still, it has its benefits. The truth is that even with some decisions firm, most of life is quite uncertain. Acknowledging this truth leads me to savor the sweetness, to suck the marrow out of those moments that I know will be gone in a blink, to know that even when I am bleary-eyed and exhausted, or frustrated beyond measure, that to be surrounded by the people I love most is a gift, and one that I am not guaranteed. In a world that is so uncertain, to have this little family is a marvel that I do not take for granted, even when the toddler has dumped an entire container of Cheerios on the dog, the general noise volume is deafening, and I've stepped on a LEGO piece for the millionth time.

It is also uncertainty that wakes me in the night, sweating from a dream in which I am in a car accident, trapped in a vehicle that is sinking fast into deep water, or searching for a lost child. It is uncertainty that makes my mind leap from bruised shin to leukemia. It is uncertainty that makes me furious when my husband neglects to respond to a text message, my mind immediately leaping to aneurysm or car accident. It is uncertainty that makes me call the pediatrician when my daughter's temperature creeps toward 101 degrees Fahrenheit. It is uncertainty that makes me take a deep breath anytime I purchase children's clothing in sizes they have yet to grow into… am I tempting fate by assuming they'll be here to wear these clothes? I wonder if I consider the worst outcome and admit the possibility of disaster (by which I mean death), can I somehow keep it from happening? Protect my family from suffering by preemptively imagining it?

It is uncertainty that urges me to bury my nose in the neck of my sleeping toddler and breathe her in. It is uncertainty that makes laundry a pleasurable chore for me—as tedious and overwhelming as it can be. I fold little girl clothes and delight in ruffle-bottom leggings and mismatched socks and sundresses because I know what it is to pack stacks of pink clothing away into bins, uncertain as to whether I would ever pull them out and use them again. Putting a load of baby clothes into the laundry before my second daughter was born was a leap of faith I couldn't take, and now pulling a warm, lavender-scented basket of t-shirts and dresses and leggings from the dryer is a comforting reassurance that they are here, stains and worn out knees as proof of life.

Uncertainty makes me second-guess decisions. It makes me cut grapes in half for my daughter who is in kindergarten. It keeps my children in rear-facing car seats longer than most. It makes me a stickler for helmets on bikes but also on scooters. Imagining worst-case scenarios seems different for those of us who are bereaved than it is for mothers who have not lost a child. Not only can we imagine it, we know what it is to have lived it. Imagining the possibility of loss isn't just a hypothetical exercise. It can bring back the visceral experience of nausea and cold sweats and heart-fluttering panic coupled with the sinking weight of grief moving from shoulders to chest. This knowledge makes me want to take all precautions in the face of uncertainty. My tolerance for risk is low. My desire for control is high.

This can be a struggle, and over the years it has certainly given me plenty to discuss with my therapist. But on the good days—and these days, most of them are good days—it also makes me treasure good-byes, each sticky embrace, each "one more kissy, Mommy!" It makes me paper the walls of my office with finger-painted masterpieces and it makes me write one line a day in a journal. I schedule annual family photographs. My Christmas tree is a time capsule. I am aware that the future is uncertain. I want to have a record of the past.

Unlike many people, I don't take it for granted that my

children will live to grow up. I see the uncertainty there. The trick is to rest in the uncertainty without letting it pull you underwater. The trick is learning to float in a sea that threatens to drown you.

Two hundred years ago, like poor Mary Shelley, women got pregnant and gave birth with much more uncertainty as to a positive outcome. I once thought such uncertainty was outdated—like corsets and polio. I thought we had moved beyond these things as a society. Now I know that no one is exempt from tragedy—no matter how hardworking, well-organized, or clean-living they might be.

Uncertainty is a curse and a blessing. For a long while, it made me reluctant to write on my calendar in advance. What was the point? Who knew what might happen? I needed therapy to help me get a grip on a life in which I was acutely and painfully aware of uncertainty. Uncertainty is closely aligned with anxiety, and managing both while also being aware of one's good fortune is one of the hardest balancing acts of all.

The key—and one I still work hard to master—is to hold uncertainty close and acknowledge its presence without feeding it so much that it grows into paralyzing fear. Uncertainty is a persistent little beast that must be acknowledged but then can be set aside. Every day is a small leap of faith, full of moments that we must trust will turn out well, as we have little to no control over viruses, other drivers, mutating cells, employer budget cuts, slippery tiles, or falling icicles. If we try to hold our breath until we've made it through all those risks, we end up gasping for air. If we can float, we can keep our faces above water.

CHAPTER 37

We know that the corollary of grief is love, and I think perhaps the antidote to anxiety is gratitude. I have always been a planner, imagining my life far into the future, but after Eliza died, I could hardly look forward at all. I didn't want to move forward without her. My future had been predictable but now it was unknowable. I had no sure footing, and I was convinced that one misstep would result in an additional loss. My therapist had me practice the art of mindfulness, of being in one moment at a time. I had to work to refocus my brain from spinning out worst case scenarios and contingency plans and instead train it to consider only the here and now. It was essentially the same advice I got early on from another mother in a forum on baby loss when I typed my desperate question, hunched over the keyboard, my throat ragged from crying, and asked how I could make it through another day without my daughter: "Breath by breath. Just take the day one breath at a time."

I am careful to distinguish between the experience

of gratitude and the assigning of a silver lining. Silver linings are dangerous things, in my opinion. For one thing, it's a trite and patronizing description of a tiny consolation in an incredibly bleak hurricane of grief. For another thing, it might allow an outsider to conclude that such loss was not as painful or as horrifying as it was because of gifts that followed. The fact is that there is nothing that can balance or replace the loss of a loved one, particularly a beloved child. There are, however, a multitude of gifts that can pile up to help offset the ache of emptiness.

One example of this is my circle of friends who are bereaved mothers. We all acknowledge frequently how grateful we are for one another, how incredibly comforting it is to have a group of friends who "gets it," how thankful we are to have had that 3 AM support through the phone or computer screen in the darkest hours of our grief. But not one of us would hesitate to drop out of this group if it meant having our child live—we've all said this to each other. If only we had met some other way—if only we'd all had living children born within a few months of each other instead of children who died within a short span of time. And yet, my gratitude for these women is immeasurable.

Now that I have living children, my greatest fear is one of them dying. At the same time, I can clearly recognize that I fear their loss because I am so incredibly grateful for their presence in my life. This gratitude for them and my desire to be the best parent for them that I can be is what makes me take a deep breath and a step back at the park when I want to hover. It is what allows me to encourage my daughter's bravery, even though watching her do a back dive into the swimming pool fills me with as much anxiety as it does pride.

My gratitude for my daughters' existence is underscored by the fear that reminds me what little control I have. All I can do is take deep breaths and try hard not to let fear overshadow the moment at hand. For me, that means not letting my grief direct the parenting choices that I make. At times, I can find myself overwhelmed because when I hear about a tragedy, a diagnosis, a freak accident, I know that my family is not safe from similar events. I know that lightning can strike twice, that great loss does not protect you from further pain, that we are all so vulnerable when we allow our hearts to love someone we can never fully protect.

But when I am at my best, I make decisions out of gratitude. Gratitude for the opportunity to sit in the sun and watch my daughter's face beam with pride as it pops out of the water after that dive. Gratitude for the opportunity to cure small boo-boos with a hug and a kiss and a Band-Aid.

In the early days of grief, gratitude was so different. I was mostly grateful for people who remembered Eliza because my greatest fear was everyone forgetting how much she matters to us. I was—and continue to be—grateful for anything that commemorates her: jewelry inscribed with her name; cards in which her name is written; text messages on her birthday every year. I was grateful for the tiniest thing that kept me tethered to this world, that kept me alive.

Still, I struggled with comprehending the senselessness of Eliza's death. Why did I even get pregnant at all? Wouldn't it have been better if I had miscarried early? I saw no reason to be grateful for a pregnancy that had ended with the death of my baby.

Shortly before I lost Eliza, my mom had given me a Christmas ornament. This was an annual tradition—she'd been buying me ornaments to represent various hobbies, interests, and activities my whole life. Even now my Christmas tree is filled with ornaments highlighting childhood interests and hobbies: the year I started taking gymnastics, the American Girl doll that I got from my grandmother, my ill-advised choice to play the trombone in middle school, my obsession with *Phantom of the Opera*. The year I was pregnant with Eliza, my mom gave me a little clay figure of a pregnant woman—brunette like me, with a round belly, holding pickles in one hand and ice cream in the other. Across the protruding clay belly, the artist had personalized it by painting "Baby Duck." It arrived a day or two before Eliza died. For many years after, I packed it away with other ornaments but I didn't take it out of the box.

For a long time, the pain of losing Eliza completely overshadowed the joy that we'd felt while expecting her. I couldn't look back at photos or read journal entries or blogs from my pregnancy because it was too painful to consider the contrast of before and after. I couldn't remember the joyful support and excitement I felt at my baby showers without those feelings being obliterated by the sickening disappointment that would follow. The ornament felt like it was mocking me, reminding me of all the hope and optimism that would come to nothing.

After a number of years, I came to see the grief as only part of the story. I can finally think of my first pregnancy and the thrill of all I anticipated as something separate from the sadness that came after. I can remember our giddy excitement with wistfulness rather than anger or shame. I can see the way that pregnancy clarified certain things for me, brought David and me closer together, linked me to a legacy of family stories and a motherhood collective, no matter how it ended. My sorrow no longer overshadows everything. But it took me a long time to get there. At long last, I began to feel grateful for the experience of my pregnancy with Eliza, even though it led to the greatest devastation of my life.

This past Christmas, I finally hung that ornament on my tree, not without an ache for what might have been, but also with gratitude for how much my first baby girl had been loved, wanted, and celebrated by my family even before she was born. I began to recognize the joy that came before the grief and the joy I can carry forward alongside it.

PART FIVE

A STORY UNFINISHED

CHAPTER 38

When I think back now to that dark night in that hospital room, the most vivid memory is fear. I was nothing but emptiness in a trembling shell, cold no matter how many warmed blankets were piled on. I was living my worst fear, and it was apparent that I would survive this tragedy and then I would have to build my life around this gaping hole in the center. I was afraid I would never recover from the trauma. I was afraid I would never have another baby. I was afraid I'd never get to raise a daughter, that my marriage would fall apart, that the isolation I was already feeling would dissolve my friendships, that I'd never have the strength or willpower to sustain a career, that my world would always be made up of this stifling fog of grief, like breathing through silt. I was afraid I would live but that everything I loved about my life would be extinguished by grief. It seemed like it would be easier to die myself.

It would have been helpful to know that I would get to the point that I didn't want to die. It would have been helpful to know that my love for Eliza could exist apart from her. It would have been helpful to know that while grief doesn't end, it does change as you learn to carry the weight of it—tilting perhaps, but on stronger and steadier legs.

I don't know if I could have believed someone who told me that I would find happiness again one day. If I could have gotten a glimpse of my future that day in December, it wouldn't have diminished my sadness, but it would have eased some of my fear.

A peek into the future would have shown me that Eliza would have three little sisters—more babies than I had ever planned! —and that Caroline, Colette, and Genevieve would all know that I wanted to be their mom because they had a sister whom I fell in love with first. I would have seen that Eliza would change my life without destroying it. I would have seen my marriage grow stronger, as imperfect as ever, but still full of love, silliness, and mutual respect. I would have seen friendships withstand the storms of my early grief, with lots of time and space for grace and forgiveness, and new friendships emerge from the shared experience of loss. I would have seen connections forged and confidence hard won from surviving what I had once declared unimaginable. I would have seen that I could emerge from the shadow of grief and carry with me the light of love for her—while also accepting that her light will always cast a shadow of grief, for that is the cost of love. I would have seen a future unfold that would not have been possible without Eliza, and I would have seen that eventually my life would become something I could love again.

I couldn't have understood at that time that my love for Eliza would not always feel like suffering. I couldn't have seen how she could be part of my story without grief taking over the entire narrative. I didn't realize at that time that I would be able to feel joy again without being disloyal to her memory. Knowing where I am now would have brought me some relief, I think, but I think it also would have been hard to swallow. It might even have felt like a betrayal. It would have shown me there was something on the other side of the suffocating heaviness of my grief, and that would have been helpful, perhaps, but I still wouldn't have known how to get through it.

Knowing that brighter days were ahead still would not have eased the sadness that closed off my throat and throbbed in my head and tied my stomach up in knots. It would not have lessened the regret I feel for the short time we had with her in the hospital. It would not have fixed the ongoing ache that comes from losing not only my baby, but also my toddler, my preschooler, my big girl, my future grown-up eldest daughter, and the wild mystery that was and will always be our Eliza. As they say, grief is love with nowhere to go, and one of the hardest things I've ever done is to have a baby and leave the hospital empty-handed, feeling completely alone in the world.

What would have helped me—what *did* help me— most of all is to know that I was not and am not alone in this experience. The only balm for grief that I could find was shared experience. Discovering grief as a universal human experience, and finding a community of parents who were living through circumstances like my own, gave me the reassurance that I was not going to be unrecognizable to myself forever, that I was not broken beyond repair, that my life would be worth living even with this sadness at the heart of it. I also discovered that I still loved Eliza, that her life was still shaping mine, that she was still an integral part of our family's story. She was my first daughter. She made me a mom.

Her death was a blight on my life, and there is no way around that hard truth. I lost easiness, innocence, a light-hearted trust in the world—but I was luckier than most to hold on to those things as long as I did. Her life has made my life more meaningful, but I'll never stop wishing that her life would have been longer, my wisdom won some other way. And yet, her life was also a gift to me in ways I could not have imagined ten years ago. Being Eliza's mom has brought immeasurable good to my life. It is never easy to hold suffering and happiness together, but like love and grief, they are two sides of the same coin.

What I did not know, and what I have discovered, is that life can be good and sweet even with deep sorrow at its heart, especially when that sorrow is rooted in an ongoing love. We who are missing our babies want them here, and if we can't have that, we want them remembered. We want everyone to see how much they matter. We want the meaning of their life and the love we poured into it to continue.

The poet Emily Dickinson—who shares her initials

with my first baby girl—wrote, "Unable are the loved to die, for love is immortality."

In that hospital room, at the lowest, darkest moment of my life, I knew that if my love could have kept her alive, it would have. And so it does. In that sense, our Eliza, like all the other babies who are deeply loved and dearly missed by their families, is very much alive in the world.

EPILOGUE

Ten Years After

As I write this, my eight-year-old is using an iPad to find LEGO sets she wants to add to her Christmas list. My six-year-old is playing "floor is lava" with pillows all over the living room. The toddler is screeching and babbling in her high chair as David makes her lunch.

This is not exactly the life I imagined when I was pregnant with Eliza—I never expected to have three living children and one dead baby.

This is not the life I imagined when Eliza died and my future felt like a black hole, every step forward a plunge into the pit of grief that had become my life.

Ten years ago, losing a baby shifted suddenly from unimaginable to unescapable. What I couldn't imagine then was how I would ever be happy again, how I would ever stop crying, how I could ever go on to have the kind of life I'd hoped for once upon a time.

Ten years after, I'm still standing. I'm eating and

drinking and walking, which was more than I could manage in those early days. I'm living that life I couldn't imagine—a life with living children, a life that has sorrow running through it, a life where painful fractures have become spaces to let light in and to spread it in more directions than I ever could have dreamed. As I think about what this means, and how Eliza continues to shape my life and my experience as a mom, what I hope my children understand is that love is big enough for grief and hope and joy. I hope that as they grow up, they realize that a beautiful life is not one untouched by grief; in fact, it may be profoundly shaped by it.

Eliza's tenth birthday—the day my first girl would have turned an entire decade old—is approaching in a few weeks. The thought of it—the might-have-beens and should-have-beens—makes my heart itch. I will always miss her. I will always wonder who she would have been. Rather than feeling emptiness, though, my life is now fuller than I would have thought possible.

This life—this life with four daughters in my heart and three in my arms, this life with more pregnancies than I had ever thought I would want, this life with a boy I met when I was twenty-one years old and thought that I had everything figured out already—this life I am living now was once unimaginable. It is both better and worse than what I dreamed of when I saw those first two pink lines on a pregnancy test on Mother's Day once upon a time. It is a life of laughter and tears and the frequently mixed up combination of both. It is a life of friendships that have sustained me and friendships that have fallen away. It is a life of heartbreaking twists of fate and unbelievable good luck. It is a life of grief and sorrow, balanced by love and joy.

If you are reading this in the darkest freefall of your grief, or after you've regained some solid footing underneath you, my wish for you is that you find your way forward by walking alongside those of us who are here with you. We are telling a story we always thought would be someone else's and we are walking a path we never wanted to find ourselves on. We are living a life that we once called *unimaginable*. And somehow, we are finding a way to make this broken life beautiful. Here we are, together.

ACKNOWLEDGEMENTS

This book could not have been written without the encouragement of my friends and fellow babyloss parents. I have so much love and gratitude for my cohort of babyloss friends who understand what it is to hold joy and grief both at once, all the time.

I want to offer my deepest thanks and biggest love:

To all those who found my blog and wrote their version of "me too" in the comments or in an email.

To those who read from the beginning and have continued to read over the years

To those who especially helped me limp through that first brutal year and my subsequent pregnancy: Sarah, Brandy, Laura, Molly, Caroline, Renel, Natasha, Julie S., Sonja, Tiffany, Julie T., Becky, Jess F., Amy, Keleen, Amelia, Veronica, Melissa, Ida, and many others whose blogs and emails I read through tear-blurred eyes, and whose babies are so loved and missed.

To Kate Inglis, who responded to my first desperate email sent in the middle of the night and told me that my writing could help to save me.

To those friends who didn't look away, who checked on me regularly, who dragged me out of the house for coffee, who brought me sandwiches even when I couldn't eat, who called and emailed and texted even when I couldn't respond.

To those friends who knew me Before and helped me remember, and who wanted to celebrate my birthday, even when I didn't and couldn't.

To those friends who met me After and remained unflinching when I dropped the bomb, and responded with their own stories and their big hearts.

To those who generously read this manuscript early and gently pointed out typos, including Heather, Michelle, and Kate.

To Dennis and Lindsey, who understand all of it.

To Monica, who showed up right away and understood when I couldn't show up for a while.

To Samantha, for her gentle but persistent encouragement, her keen eye as an early reader, and all her writing advice.

To all our family members who never fail to remember Eliza.

To my mom and dad, who are indisputably the best Grammy and Bops, and my brother and sister-in-law, who love and miss Eliza with us.

And, of course, to my partner, my teammate, and my favorite, David, who makes this unimaginable life possible and without whom I wouldn't have what I love most in this world: Zuzu, Coco, and Gee. My baby ducks.

Made in the USA
Las Vegas, NV
06 May 2021

22564610R10150